ool
ve
he
ed
on the stage in 1954 at the Preston Repertory Theatre in a play with the unlikely title *The Gay Dog*. He made his first London appearance in *Free As Air* at the Savoy. Since then he has starred in the West End, at the Old Vic, and on Broadway in a wide range of plays including the notable Brecht *Arturo Ui* for which he won a variety of awards.

Leonard Rossiter has made hundreds of appearances on television and has become a household name through the tremendous success of *The Rise and Fall of Reginald Perrin* on BBC and *Rising Damp* on ITV – the film of which has now been released.

THE DEVIL'S BEDSIDE BOOK

Compiled by
LEONARD ROSSITER

Hamlyn Paperbacks

THE DEVIL'S BEDSIDE BOOK
ISBN 0 600 20105 8

First published
in Great Britain 1980
by Hamlyn Paperbacks

Reprinted 1980

Hamlyn Paperbacks are published by
The Hamlyn Publishing Group Ltd,
Astronaut House,
Feltham,
Middlesex, England

(Paperback Division: Hamlyn Paperbacks,
Banda House, Cambridge Grove,
Hammersmith, London W6 0LE)

Set, printed and bound in Great Britain by
Cox & Wyman Ltd, Reading

Dedicated to Vicky and Honey, the
two Abyssinians who share my life.*

*Don't worry: they're only cats.

THE DEVIL'S BEDSIDE BOOK

CONTENTS

ACKNOWLEDGEMENTS

The material in the section 'The Devil's Dictionary' represents only a fraction of what Ambrose Bierce wrote. If you want to read more from the master of diabolical definitions I recommend *The Enlarged Devil's Dictionary*, edited by Ernest Hopkins (Victor Gollancz Ltd, London, 1967).

In compiling 'The Devil's Laws' I drew on a variety of sources and gratefully thank the following for permission to reproduce their material:

Murphy's Law and its corollaries:
Murphy's Law and Other Reasons Why Things Go Wrong, Arthur Bloch (Price, Stern, Sloan Publishers Inc., California, 1977; Magnum Books, London, 1979).

Parkinson's First, Second, Third, Fourth, Fifth Laws, Parkinson's Law of Delay and Parkinson's Axioms:
Parkinson's Law, 1958, *Mrs Parkinson's Law*, 1968, *The Law and the Profits*, 1960, *The Law of Delay*, 1970, and *In-laws and Outlaws*, 1962, C. Northcote Parkinson (John Murray, London).

The Peter Principle, Peter's Inversion, Peter's Law of Substitution, Peter's Observation, Peter's Placebo, Peter's Prognosis, Peter's Rule for Creative Incompetence:
The Peter Principle, Laurence J. Peter and Raymond Hull (William Morrow, New York, 1969; Souvenir Press Ltd, London 1967).

Eddington's Theory, Maier's Law, Old and Kahn's Law, Parkinson's Law for Medical Research, Peter's Hidden Postulate, First, Second, Third, Fourth, Fifth, Sixth Laws of Procrastination, A Law of Sociogenetics, Spark's Rule for Managers:
Journal of Irreproducible Results (Chicago Heights, Illinois, 1955–79).

Experimenter's Data Law:
'Science Conquers All', L. Aurelian, in *Intellectual Digest* 4:47 (March, 1974).
Experimenter's Law of Animal Behaviour and Bromily's Maxim:
'What Psychology is About', D. O. Hebb, in *American Psychologist* 29:71–79 (February, 1974).
Fetridge's Law, Gumperson's Law:
A Short History of Fingers (and Other State Papers), H. A. Smith (Little, Brown and Company, Boston, 1963).
Agnes Allen's Law, Colonel Stapp's Ironical Paradox and Smith's Law:
'The Lawful Truth', J. Smith, in *Los Angeles Times*, part 4 page 1 (13 January 1977).

INTRODUCTION

I've not yet met the Devil in person and, between you and me, I confess I'm hoping I never shall. I think I could probably cope if he looked like the devil of the Victorian pantomime stage, complete with horns, forked tail and maniacal grin, but I'm rather afraid he won't turn out to look like someone who's got lost on their way to a Fancy Dress Ball at all. He'll be much more sinister. I suspect that when you open the door of Hell, the Devil that greets you is your very best friend, the person dearest and closest to you – and that would be the horror of Hell: it's your loved ones who are your torturers there. And since mental anguish is far worse than physical suffering I've no doubt the real agony of Hell won't be burning fires but having all the secret humiliations of your life played back to you in perpetuity and in stereo!

That makes me sound rather morbid, which I'm not, despite the fact that one of the things I like most about my house is that it overlooks a cemetery – Brompton Cemetery, one of the largest and most intriguing of London's Victorian cemeteries, covering about thirty-eight acres and housing the graves of all sorts of famous people. Emmeline Pankhurst, the suffragette, is buried there; and Percy E. Lambert the motor-racing pioneer, who was the first man to cover one hundred miles in one hour at Brooklands. He was killed on the track in 1913 and now he's lying outside my bedroom window. Richard Tauber, the great singer, is there too, and Brandon Thomas who wrote the marvellous farce *Charley's Aunt*. Like Samuel Beckett, 'I have no bone to pick with graveyards, I take the air there willingly', and I love to read the epitaphs. One of the most eloquent is on the monument over the grave of Robert Coombes, a Thames waterman and champion sculler who died in a lunatic asylum in 1860. It reads:

Fare thee well my trim-built wherry.
Oars, coat and badge, farewell.

The most touching tombstone epitaph I've ever come across isn't in Brompton Cemetery. It's one that an actor friend of mine, Jeremy Kemp, told me he had seen in a Suffolk churchyard. Inscribed on the gravestone of a child who had died aged eighteen months were the words:

Came in,
Walked about,
Didn't like it,
Walked out.

I think that shows a marvellously philosophical attitude to death on the part of that child's parents. And – turning from the sublime to the ridiculous – I think that what you're going to find in this book shows a marvellously philosophical attitude to *life*.

I love life and don't look forward to death at all. I could certainly never do what some Americans do and book my burial plot in advance. Not long ago I visited the amazing Forest Lawn cemetery in California where alongside 'nuclear-proof mausoleums' you can actually see the graves that perfectly healthy people have already reserved for themselves! The tombstones are almost complete:

HARRY FINKELBAUM (1892–1961)
MARY FINKELBAUM (1903–   )

All you have to do when the time comes is add the coffin and the date. It's almost as bad as putting one of those blue plaques on the outside of your house saying 'WATCH THIS SPACE'.

No, I'm not looking forward to meeting the Devil after death. But that doesn't mean to say I'm not prepared to enlist his services while I'm still alive! There can be no doubt that the sayings and laws I have collected here are pretty devilish, but they are not intended to provide you with a passport to Hell! Far from it. The idea is to give you a vade-mecum, a diabolical bedside book designed to help you get through life in this world and keep your mind off life in the next.

THE DEVIL'S DICTIONARY

According to the *Guinness Book of Records* the world's largest dictionary is the twelve-volume *Oxford English Dictionary* first published between 1884 and 1928. According to yours truly the world's most unique dictionary is the *Devil's Dictionary* first published between 1881 and 1911. It is the work of one of America's most original men of letters, Ambrose Gwinnet Bierce, who was born on 24 June 1842 in Meigs County, Ohio. He was the son of a farmer and, as he never went to school, what education he got came from reading his father's books. When he left home he went to work for the Mint in San Francisco and it was then that he began writing articles for local weeklies. In 1871 his first short story – 'The Haunted Valley' – was published. On Christmas Day of that year he married, and sailed for England where he joined the staff of the journal *Fun* and began publishing humorous writings. He was a very funny writer – a great satirist in the tradition of Mark Twain – but not a happy man. In 1913, at the age of seventy-one, he left for Mexico 'with a pretty definite purpose, which, however, is not at present disclosable'. He was never heard from again. But his memorial remains in the form of his extraordinary *Devil's Dictionary* from which the gems that follow are culled. It is addressed to those enlightened souls who prefer dry wines to sweet, sense to sentiment, and wit to humour.

I like these 'diabolical definitions' so much because though they may be cynical they are in no sense snide. I like them too because although Bierce was very much an American his observations are universal. He takes an amused, detached look at life that is sometimes hilarious and always refreshing. The best of the definitions are those that ring truest.

Accuser. One's former friend; particularly the person for whom one has performed some friendly service.

How true! I remember hearing Harold Macmillan saying on television once that President de Gaulle could never forgive the British for saving France! People *do* resent too big a favour.

What I admire most about Bierce is the way he manages to get straight to the heart of the matter. Look at his definition of cribbage, for example: 'A substitute for conversation among those to whom nature has denied ideas.'

It's brilliant. It hits the nail right on the head. I don't play cribbage myself but I do play poker so I know what I'm talking about. (My wife plays *bridge* but that requires too much subtle forward-planning for my liking. It's like chess. My brother was a brilliant chess player, but I have never mastered the game. If I can think of two moves ahead I'm doing well; but the real experts manage to play the whole game in their heads virtually before they start! I am inclined to agree with Byron – not Lord Byron, the poet, but H. J. Byron the Victorian playwright, who also happens to be buried in the cemetery behind my house – who once said, 'Life's too short for chess'. But enough of these asides – back to Bierce!)

Here is another of my favourites:

> **Abuse.** Unanswerable wit.

There actually are people who can transform abuse into unanswerable wit. Unfortunately I am not one of them. I long for pearls of acid wisdom to come cascading from my lips, but somehow they don't. My wife Gillian says I'm argumentative – I disagree! – but even when my invective is effective it's very rarely witty. And, inevitably, when I most need to have a caustic riposte at the ready, I'm totally at a loss for words.

When I was a child I used to play the recorder and recently I thought how nice it would be to take up the piano. My seven-year-old daughter is learning to play and I felt it would be fun if we could practise duets together. Well, the other day I was at a party at Susan Hampshire's house and I met Benny Green. I thought, here's a man who knows a lot about music, so I ventured to mention that I was thinking of taking up the piano and asked him how he thought I'd get on. He didn't give me a straight answer. In fact he didn't say a thing. He just laughed and laughed and laughed. He's such a nice bloke that eventually I joined in the laughter. But if I'd only had some 'unanswerable wit' to offer, how much more impressive!

If you have a good memory you might try memorizing some of Bierce's diabolical definitions to trot them out whenever the need arises. The best ones are very like Bob Hope one-liners! But if you don't happen to have a good memory, don't despair. As someone once said, 'Silence is the unbearable repartee.'

FROM BIERCE . . .

Abasement. A decent and customary mental attitude in the presence of wealth or power. Peculiarly appropriate in an employee when addressing an employer.

Abbess. A female father.

Abdication. An act whereby a sovereign attests his sense of the high temperature of the throne.

Aberration. Any deviation in another from one's own habit of thought, not sufficient in itself to constitute insanity.

Abhorrence. One of the degrees of disapproval due to what is imperfectly understood.

Ability. The natural equipment to accomplish some small part of the meaner ambitions distinguishing able men from dead ones. In the last analysis ability is commonly found to consist mainly in a high degree of solemnity. Perhaps, however, this impressive quality is rightly appraised; it is no easy task to be solemn.

Abnormal. Not conforming to standard. In matters of thought and conduct, to be independent is to be abnormal, to be abnormal is to be detested.

Abominable. The quality of another's opinions.

Abridgement. A brief summary of some person's literary work, in which those parts that tell against the convictions of the abridger are omitted for want of space.

Abroad. At war with savages and idiots. To be a Frenchman abroad is to be miserable; to be an American abroad is to make others miserable.

Abrupt. Sudden, without ceremony, like the arrival of a cannon-shot and the departure of the soldier whose interests are most affected by it.

Abscond. To 'move in a mysterious way', commonly with the property of another.

Absence. That which 'makes the heart grow fonder' – of absence. Absence of mind is the cerebral condition essential to success in popular preaching. It is sometimes termed lack of sense.

Absent. Peculiarly exposed to the teeth of detraction; vilified; hopelessly in the wrong; superseded in the consideration and affection of another.

Absolute. Independent, irresponsible. An absolute monarchy is one in which the sovereign does as he pleases so long as he pleases the assassins. Not many absolute monarchies are left, most of them having been replaced by limited monarchies, where the sovereign's power for evil (and for good) is greatly curtailed, and by republics, which are governed by chance.

Abstainer. A weak person who yields to the temptation of denying himself a pleasure. A total abstainer is one who abstains from everything but abstention, and especially from inactivity in the affairs of others.

Abstemious. Thoughtfully deferential to one's overtaxed capacity.

Absurdity. A statement or belief manifestly inconsistent with one's own opinion.

Abuse. Unanswerable wit.

Accident. An inevitable occurrence due to the action of immutable natural laws.

Accomplice. One associated with another in crime, having guilty knowledge and complicity, as an attorney who defends a criminal, knowing him guilty. This view of the attorney's position in the matter has not hitherto commanded the assent of attorneys, no-one having offered them a fee for assenting.

Accountable. Liable to an abatement of pleasure, profit or advantage; exposed to the peril of a penalty.

Accuracy. A certain uninteresting quality carefully excluded from human statements.

Accuse. To affirm another's guilt or unworth; most commonly as a justification of ourselves for having wronged him.

Accuser. One's former friend; particularly the person for whom one has performed some friendly service.

Achievement. The death of endeavour and the birth of disgust.

Acknowledge. To confess. Acknowledgement of one another's faults is the highest duty imposed by our love of truth.

Acquaintance. A person whom we know well enough to borrow from, but not well enough to lend to. A degree of friendship called slight when its object is poor or obscure, and intimate when he is rich or famous.

Actor. One who peddles ready-made emotion, and who, despising us for the qualities upon which he feeds, is by us despised for the unwholesome character of his diet.

Actually. Perhaps; possibly.

Adam's Apple. A protuberance in the throat of man, thoughtfully provided by Nature to keep the rope in place.

Adder. A species of snake. So called from its habit of adding funeral outlays to the other expenses of living.

Adherent. A follower who has not yet obtained all that he expects to get.

Admirability. My kind of ability, as distinguished from your kind of ability.

Admiral. That part of a warship which does the talking while the figure-head does the thinking.

Admiration. Our polite recognition of another's resemblance to ourselves.

Admonition. Gentle reproof, as with a meat-axe. Friendly warning.

Adolescent. Recovering from boyhood.

Affectionate. Addicted to being a nuisance. The most affectionate creature in the world is a wet dog.

Affirm. To declare with suspicious gravity when one is not compelled to wholly discredit oneself with an oath.

Afraid. Civilly willing that things should be other than they seem.

Agony. A superior degree of bodily disgust.

Alliance. In international politics, the union of two thieves who have their hands so deeply inserted in each other's pocket that they cannot separately plunder a third.

Alone. In bad company.

Amateur. A public nuisance who mistakes taste for skill, and confounds his ambition with his ability.

Amazon. One of an ancient race who do not appear to have been much concerned about woman's rights and the equality of the sexes. Their thoughtless habit of twisting the necks of the males has unfortunately resulted in the extinction of their kind.

Ambidextrous. Able to pick a pocket with either hand.

Ambition. An overmastering desire to be vilified by enemies while living and made ridiculous by friends when dead.

Amnesty. The state's magnanimity to those offenders whom it would be too expensive to punish.

Antipathy. The sentiment inspired by one's friend's friend.

Apathetic. Six weeks married.

Aphorism. Predigested wisdom.

Apologize. To lay the foundation for a future offence.

Appeal. In law, to put the dice into the box for another throw.

Applause. The echo of a platitude.

Architect. One who drafts a plan of your house, and plans a draft of your money.

Ardour. The quality that distinguishes love without knowledge.

Arena. In politics, an imaginary rat-pit in which the statesman wrestles with his record.

Aristocracy. Government by the best men. (In this sense the word is obsolete; so is that kind of government.)

Armour. The kind of clothing worn by a man whose tailor is a blacksmith.

Arrest. Formally to detain one accused of unusualness.

Arrested. Caught criming without the money to satisfy the policeman.

Astrology. The science of making the dupe see stars. Astrology is by some held high in respect as the precursor of astronomy.

Australia. A country lying in the South Sea, whose industrial and commercial development has been unspeakably retarded by an unfortunate dispute among geographers as to whether it is a continent or an island.

Authentic. Indubitably true – in somebody's opinion.

Avenge. In modern usage, to take satisfaction for an injury by cheating the inflictor.

Baby. A misshapen creature of no particular age, sex, or condition, chiefly remarkable for the violence of the sympathies and antipathies it excites in others, itself without sentiment or emotion.

Bacchus. A convenient deity invented by the ancients as an excuse for getting drunk.

Bachelor. A man whom women are still sampling.

Bacon. To 'save one's bacon' is to narrowly escape some particular woman, or other peril.

Bald. Destitute of hair from hereditary or accidental causes – never from age.

Ballot. A simple device by which a majority proves to a minority the folly of resistance. Many worthy persons of imperfect thinking apparatus believe that majorities govern through some inherent right; and that minorities submit, not because they must, but because they ought.

Bandit. A person who takes by force from A what A has taken by guile from B.

Bard. A person who makes rhymes. The word is one of the numerous aliases under which the poet seeks to veil his identity and escape opprobrium.

Barometer. An ingenious instrument which indicates what kind of weather we are having.

Barrister. One of the ten thousand varieties of the genus *Lawyer*. In England the functions of a barrister are distinct from those of a solicitor. The one advises; the other executes. But the thing advised and the thing executed is the client.

Beggar. A pest unkindly inflicted on the suffering rich. Also, one who has relied on the assistance of his friends.

Belladonna. In Italian a beautiful lady; in English a deadly poison. A striking example of the essential identity of the two tongues.

Bequeath. To generously give to another that which can no longer be denied to *somebody*.

Betrothed. The condition of a man and woman who, pleasing to one another and objectionable to their friends, are anxious to propitiate society by becoming unendurable to each other.

Bigamy. A mistake in taste for which the wisdom of the future will adjudge a punishment called trigamy.

Bigot. One who is obstinately and zealously attached to an opinion that you do not entertain.

Birth. The first and direst of all disasters. As to the nature of it there appears to be no uniformity. Castor and Pollux were born from the egg. Pallas came out of a skull. Galatea was once a block of stone. Peresilis, who wrote in the tenth century, avers that he grew up out of the ground where a priest had spilled holy water. It is known that Arimaxus was derived from a hole in the earth, made by a stroke of lightning. Leucomedon was the son of a cavern in Mount Aetna, and I have myself seen a man come out of a wine cellar.

Blushing. A trick formerly in great favour with women, but now fallen into disuse as a lost art, though by laborious practice the modern damsel is still able to achieve it at the risk of being taken in hand and treated for apoplexy.

Book-learning. The dunce's derisive term for all knowledge that transcends his own impenitent ignorance.

Bore. A person who talks when you wish him to listen.

Brain. An apparatus with which we think that we think. That which distinguishes the man who is content to *be* something from the man who wishes to *do* something. A man of great wealth, or one who has been pitchforked into high station, has commonly such a headful of brain that his neighbours cannot keep their hats on.

Bribe. That which enables a member of a legislature to live on his pay without any dishonest economies.

Bride. A woman with a fine prospect of happiness behind her.

Cabbage. A familiar kitchen-garden vegetable about as large and wise as a man's head.

Cabinet. The principal persons charged with the mismanagement of a government, the charge commonly being well founded.

Cadet. A young military gentleman who ten years hence may be shaking the world and cutting the throats of nations.

Calamity. A more than commonly plain and unmistakable reminder that the affairs of this life are not of our own ordering. Calamities are of two kinds: misfortune to ourselves, and good fortune to others.

Callous. Gifted with great fortitude to bear the evils afflicting another.

Candidate. One who by the advice of his friends reluctantly consents to sacrifice his private interests to the public good.

Cannibal. A gastronome of the old school who preserves the simple test and adheres to the natural diet of the pre-pork period.

Capital. The seat of misgovernment.

Carnivorous. Addicted to the cruelty of devouring the timorous vegetarian, his heirs and assigns.

Carouse. To celebrate with appropriate ceremonies the birth of a noble headache.

Cartesian. Relating to Descartes, a famous philosopher, author of the celebrated dictum '*cogito ergo sum*', whereby he was pleased to suppose he demonstrated the reality of human existence. The dictum might be improved, however, thus: '*cogito cogito ergo cogito sum*' – 'I think that I think, therefore I think that I am'; as close an approach to certainty as any philosopher has yet made.

Cat. A soft indestructible automaton provided by nature to be kicked when things go wrong in the domestic circle.

Cenotaph. A tomb from which the body is absent, living elsewhere. The grave whose headstone bore the famous inscription:

Here lies me two children dear,
One in ould Ireland, t'other one here

was a cenotaph, so far as regarded the 'one in ould Ireland'.

Censor. An officer of certain governments, employed to suppress the works of genius. Among the Romans the censor was an inspector of public morals, but the public morals of modern nations will not bear inspection.

Charity. An amiable quality of the heart which moves us to condone in others the sins and vices to which we ourselves are addicted.

Child. An accident to the occurrence of which all the forces and arrangements of nature are specially devised and accurately adapted.

Childhood. The period of human life intermediate between the idiocy of infancy and the folly of youth – two removes from the sin of manhood and three from the remorse of age.

Chop. A piece of leather skilfully attached to a bone and administered to the patients at restaurants.

Chorus. In opera, a band of howling dervishes who terrify the audience while the singers are taking breath.

Christen. To ceremoniously afflict a helpless child with a name.

Christian. One who believes that the New Testament is a divinely inspired book admirably suited to the spiritual needs of his neighbour. One who follows the teachings of Christ in so far as they are not inconsistent with a life of sin.

Christmas. A day set apart and consecrated to gluttony, drunkenness, maudlin sentiment, gift-taking, public dullness and domestic behaviour.

Circumlocution. A literary trick whereby the writer who has nothing to say breaks it gently to the reader.

Circus. A place where horses, ponies and elephants are permitted to see men, women and children acting the fool.

Clock. A machine of great moral value to man, allaying his concern for the future by reminding him what a lot of time remains to him.

Close-fisted. Unduly desirous of keeping that which many meritorious persons wish to obtain.

Comfort. A state of mind produced by contemplation of a neighbour's uneasiness.

Commendation. The tribute that we pay to achievements that resemble, but do not equal, our own.

Commerce. A kind of transaction in which A plunders from B the goods of C, and for compensation B picks the pocket of D of money belonging to E.

Competitor. A scoundrel who desires that which *we* desire.

Compromise. Such an adjustment of conflicting interests as gives each adversary the satisfaction of thinking he has got what he ought not to have, and is deprived of nothing except what was justly his due.

Concession. A lowering of one's guard to elicit an adversary's ill-considered thrust.

Confidant. One entrusted by A with the secrets of B, confided to *him* by C.

Congratulation. The civility of envy.

Connoisseur. A specialist who knows everything about something and nothing about anything else.

An old wine-bibber having been smashed in a railway collision, some wine was poured upon his lips to revive him. 'Pauillac, 1873,' he murmured, and died.

Conscience. A morbid condition of the stomach, affecting the grey matter of the brain and producing a mental discord.

Conservative. A statesman who is enamoured of existing evils, as distinguished from the Liberal, who wishes to replace them with others.

Consolation. The knowledge that a better man is more unfortunate than yourself.

Consult. To seek another's approval of a course already decided on.

Contempt. The feeling of a prudent man for an enemy who is too formidable safely to be opposed.

Conversation. A fair for the display of the minor mental commodities, each exhibitor being too intent upon the arrangement of his own wares to observe those of his neighbour.

Cookery. A household art and practice of making unpalatable that which was already indigestible.

Coroner. A municipal officer charged with the duty of cutting up the unfortunate to see if they are dead. They always are.

Corporation. An ingenious device for obtaining individual profit without individual responsibility.

Corpse. A person who manifests the highest possible degree of indifference that is consistent with a civil regard for the solicitude of others.

Corrupt. In politics, holding an office of trust or profit.

Courtship. The timid sipping of two thirsty souls from a goblet which both can easily drain but neither replenish.

Coward. One who in a perilous emergency thinks with his legs.

Coyness. A species of reluctance formerly affected by young women but now abandoned as 'bad form'.

Craft. A fool's substitute for brains.

Cremation. The process by which the cold meats of humanity are warmed over.

Cribbage. A substitute for conversation among those to whom nature has denied ideas.

Culprit. The other fellow.

Cunning. The faculty that distinguishes a weak animal or person from a strong one. It brings its possessor much mental satisfaction and great material adversity.

Cynic. A blackguard whose faulty vision sees things as they are, not as they ought to be. Hence the custom among the Scythians of plucking out a cynic's eyes to improve his vision.

Dance. To leap about to the sound of tittering music, preferably with arms about your neighbour's wife or daughter.

Darling. The bore of opposite sex in an early stage of development.

Dawn. The time when men of reason go to bed. Certain old men prefer to rise at about that time, taking a cold bath and a long walk with an empty stomach, and otherwise mortifying the flesh. They then point with pride to these practices as the cause of their sturdy health and ripe years; the truth being that they are hearty and old, not because of their habits, but in spite of them. The reason we find only robust persons doing this thing is that it has killed all the others who have tried it.

Day. A period of twenty-four hours, mostly misspent. This period is divided into two parts, the day proper and the night, or day improper – the former devoted to sins of business, the latter consecrated to the other sort. These two kinds of social activity overlap.

Debauchee. One who has so earnestly pursued pleasure that he has had the misfortune to overtake it.

Decanter. A vessel whose functions are most envied by the human stomach.

Decide. To succumb to the preponderance of one set of influences over another.

Defame. To lie about another. To tell the truth about another.

Defenceless. Unable to attack.

Degenerate. Less conspicuously admirable than one's ancestors.

Deist. One who believes in God, but reserves the right to worship the devil.

Demagogue. A political opponent.

Demented. The melancholy mental condition of one whose arguments we are unable to answer.

Dentist. A prestidigitator, who puts metal into your mouth and pulls coins out of your pocket.

Deposit. A charitable contribution to the support of a bank.

Depraved. The moral condition of a gentleman who holds the opposite opinion.

Depression. The state of mind produced by a newspaper joke, a minstrel performance, or the contemplation of another's success.

Derision. The ineffectual argument by which a fool imagines he has answered the contempt of the wise.

Destiny. A force alleged to control affairs, principally quoted by erring human beings to excuse their failures.

Devil. The author of all our woes and proprietor of all the good things of this world. He was made by the Almighty, but brought into the world by a woman.

Devotion. A mild type of mental aberration variously produced; in love, by a surplus of blood; in religion, by chronic dyspepsia.

Diaphragm. A muscular partition separating disorders of the chest from disorders of the bowels.

Dice. Small polka-dotted cubes of ivory, constructed like a lawyer to lie on any side, but commonly on the wrong one.

Dictator. The chief of a nation that prefers the pestilence of despotism to the plague of anarchy.

Dictionary. A malevolent literary device for cramping the growth of a language and making it hard and inelastic.

Dine. To eat a good dinner in good company, and eat it slow. In dining, as distinguished from mere feeding, the palate and stomach never ask the hand, 'What are you giving us?'

Diplomacy. The patriotic art of lying for one's country.

Disabuse. To present your neighbour with another and better error than the one which he has deemed it advantageous to embrace.

Discreditable. In the characteristic and customary manner of a rival.

Discriminate. To note the particulars in which one person or thing is, if possible, more objectionable than another.

Dishonesty. An important element of commercial success, to which the best business colleges have not as yet accorded an honourable prominence in the curriculum, but have weakly substituted penmanship.

Dispatches. A complete account of all the murders, outrages, and other disgusting crimes which take place everywhere, disseminated daily by an Associated Press for the amelioration of the world in general.

Distance. The only thing that the rich are willing for the poor to call theirs, and keep.

Divorce. A resumption of diplomatic relations and rectification of boundaries.

Doctor. A gentleman who thrives upon disease and dies of health.

Drunk. Boozy, fuddled, corned, tipsy, mellow, soaked, full, groggy, tired, top-heavy, glorious, overcome, swipy, elevated, overtaken, screwed, raddled, lushy, nappy, muzzy, maudlin, pious, floppy, loppy, happy, etc.

Duty. That which sternly impels us in the direction of profit, along the line of desire.

Eavesdrop. Secretly to overhear a catalogue of the crimes and vices of another or yourself.

Eccentricity. A method of distinction so cheap that fools employ it to accentuate their incapacity.

Education. That which discloses to the wise and disguises from the foolish their lack of understanding.

Effect. The second of two phenomena which always occur together in the same order. The first, called a Cause, is said to generate the other – which is no more sensible that it would be for one who has never seen a dog except in pursuit of a rabbit to declare the rabbit the cause of the dog.

Egotist. A person of low taste, more interested in himself than me.

Elector. One who enjoys the sacred privilege of voting for the man of another man's choice.

Eloquence. The art of orally persuading fools that white is the colour that it appears to be. It includes the gift of making any colour appear white.

Emergency. The wise man's opportunity and the fool's Waterloo. A condition of things requiring one to think like a millstream, look like an idiot and act like an earthquake.

Emotion. A prostrating disease caused by a determination of the heart to the head. It is sometimes accompanied by a copious discharge of hydrated chloride of sodium from the eyes.

Encourage. To confirm a fool in a folly that is beginning to hurt him.

Enemy. A designing scoundrel who has done you some service which it is inconvenient to repay. In military affairs, a body of men actuated by the basest motives and pursuing the most iniquitous aim.

English. A language so haughty and reserved that few writers succeed in getting on terms of familiarity with it.

Epitaph. A monumental inscription designed to remind the deceased of what might have been if he had had the will and the opportunity.

Equal. As bad as something else.

Esoteric. Very particularly abstruse and consummately occult. The ancient philosophies were of two kinds – 'exoteric', those that the philosophers themselves could partly understand, and 'esoteric', those that nobody could understand. It is the latter that have most profoundly affected modern thought and found greatest acceptance in our time.

Esteem. The degree of favourable regard that is due to one who has the power to serve us and has not yet refused.

Etiquette. A code of social rites, ceremonies and observances, constituting a vulgarian's claim to toleration. The fool's credentials.

Euchre. A game of cards in which the highest cards and the best players are knaves.

Eulogy. Praise of a person who has either the advantages of wealth and power, or the consideration to be dead.

Euphemism. A figure of speech in which the speaker or writer makes his expression a good deal softer than the facts would warrant him in doing.

Exception. A thing which takes the liberty to differ from other things of its class, as, an honest man, a truthful woman, etc. 'The exception proves the rule', is an expression constantly upon the lips of the ignorant, who parrot it with never a thought of its absurdity. In the Latin, '*Exceptio probat regulam*' means that the exception tests the rule, puts it to the proof, not confirms it. The malefactor who drew the meaning from this excellent dictum and substituted a contrary one of his own exerted an evil power which appears to be immortal.

Excursion. An expedition of so disagreeable a character that steamboat and railroad fares are compassionately mitigated to the miserable sufferers.

Exile. One who serves his country by residing abroad, yet is not an ambassador.

Expectation. The state or condition of mind which in the procession of human emotions is preceded by Hope and followed by Despair.

Experience. The wisdom that enables us to recognize as an undesirable old acquaintance the folly that we have already embraced.

Faith. Belief without evidence in what is told by one who speaks without knowledge, of things without parallel.

Falsehood. A truth to which the facts are loosely adjusted to an imperfect conformity.

Family. A body of individuals living in one household, consisting of male, female, young, servants, dog, cat, dicky-bird, cockroaches, bedbugs and fleas – the 'unit' of modern civilized society.

Famous. Conspicuously miserable.

Fatigue. The condition of a philosopher after having considered human wisdom and virtue.

Fault. One of my offences, as distinguished from one of yours, the latter being crimes.

Female. One of the opposing or unfair sex.

Finance. The art or science of managing revenues and resources for the best advantage of the manager.

Foe. A person instigated by his wicked nature to deny one's merits or exhibit superior merits of his own.

Fool. A person who pervades the domain of intellectual speculation and diffuses himself through the channels of moral activity. He it was who invented letters, printing, the railroad, the steamboat, the telegraph, the platitude and the circle of the sciences. He created patriotism and taught the nations war – founded theology, philosophy, law, medicine and Chicago. He established monarchical and republican government. He is from everlasting to everlasting – such as creation's dawn beheld he fooleth now. And after the rest of us shall have retired for the night of eternal oblivion he will sit up to write a history of human civilization.

Foolhardy. Unlucky in the execution of a courageous act.

Forbidden. Invested with a new and irresistible charm.

Foreign. Belonging to another and inferior country.

Foreigner. A villain regarded with various and varying degrees of toleration, according to his conformity to the eternal standard of our conceit and the shifting one of our interests. Among the Romans all foreigners were called barbarians because most of the tribes with which the Romans had acquaintance were bearded. The term was merely descriptive, having nothing of reproach in it; Roman disparagement was generally more frankly expressed with a spear.

Forgiveness. A stratagem to throw an offender off his guard and catch him red-handed in his next offence.

Fork. An instrument used chiefly for the purpose of putting dead animals into the mouth.

Fraud. The life of commerce, the soul of religion, the bait of courtship and the basis of political power.

Friendless. Having no favours to bestow. Destitute of fortune. Addicted to utterance of truth and common sense.

Funeral. A pageant whereby we attest our respect for the dead by enriching the undertaker, and strengthen our grief by an expenditure that deepens our groans and doubles our tears.

Future. That period of time in which our affairs prosper, our friends are true and our happiness is assured.

Gambling. A pastime in which the pleasure consists partly in the consciousness of advantages gained for oneself, but mainly in the contemplation of another's loss.

Gent. The male of the genus *Hoodlum.*

Gentleman. A rare animal.

Gentlewoman. The female of the genus *Gentleman.*

Genuine. Real, veritable. As, a genuine counterfeit, genuine hypocrisy, etc.

Gipsy. A person who is willing to tell your fortune for a small portion of it.

Glutton. A person who escapes the evils of moderation by committing dyspepsia.

Gold. A yellow metal greatly prized for its convenience in the various kinds of robbery known as trade. The word was formerly spelled 'God' – the 'l' was inserted to distinguish it from the name of another, and inferior, deity.

Grammar. A system of pitfalls thoroughly prepared for the feet of the self-made man, along the path of which he advances to distinction.

Gravitation. The tendency of all bodies to approach one

another with a strength proportional to the quantity of matter they contain – the quantity of matter they contain being ascertained by the strength of their tendency to approach one another. This is a lovely and edifying illustration of how science, having made A the proof of B, makes B the proof of A.

Guardian. One who undertakes to protect others from what he is not ready to get for himself.

Guillotine. A machine which makes a Frenchman shrug his shoulders with good reason.

Guilt. The condition of one who is known to have committed an indiscretion, as distinguished from the state of him who has covered his tracks.

Guinea. A coin of twenty-one shillings, formerly minted in Great Britain, and still used as the unit of computation in fees for professional services, bribes and other transactions between gentlemen.

Gymnast. A man who puts his brains into his muscles.

Hammer. An instrument for smashing the human thumb.

Handkerchief. A small square of silk or linen, used in various ignoble offices about the face and especially serviceable at funerals to conceal the lack of tears.

Hangman. An officer who produces suspended animation.

Happiness. An agreeable sensation arising from contemplating the misery of another.

Harangue. A political speech by an opponent.

Hatred. A sentiment appropriate to the occasion of another's superiority.

Haughty. Proud and disdainful, like a waiter.

Head. That portion of the human body which is supposed to be responsible for all the others. It is customary in some countries to remove it, and many have acquired great skill and proficiency in the art.

Heart. An automatic muscular bloodpump. Figuratively, this useful organ is said to be the seat of emotions and sentiments – a very pretty fancy which, however, is nothing but a survival of a once universal belief. It is now known that the sentiments and emotions reside in the stomach.

Heathen. A benighted creature who has the folly to worship something that he can see and feel.

Heaven. A place where the wicked cease from troubling you with talk of their personal affairs, and the good listen with attention while you expound your own.

Hedgehog. The cactus of the animal kingdom.

Hermit. A person whose vices and follies are not sociable.

Hireling. A mercenary wretch who serves another person for wages, as distinguished from the respectable functionary who receives a salary.

Historian. A broad-gauge gossip.

Home. The place of last resort – open all night.

Homesick. Dead broke abroad.

Homicide. The slaying of one human being by another. There are four kinds of homicide: felonious, excusable, justifiable and praiseworthy, but it makes no great difference to the person slain whether he fell by one kind or another – the classification is for advantage of the lawyers.

Honest. Afflicted with an impediment in his dealing.

Hope. Desire and expectation rolled into one.

Hospitality. The virtue which induces us to feed and lodge certain persons who are not in need of food and lodging.

House. A hollow edifice erected for the habitation of man, rat, mouse, beetle, cockroach, fly, mosquito, bacillus and microbe.

House of Correction – a place of reward for political and personal service, and for the detention of offenders and appropriations.

House of God – a building with a steeple and a mortgage on it.

House-dog – a pestilent beast kept on domestic premises to insult persons passing by and appal the hardy visitor.

Housemaid – a youngerly person of the opposing sex employed to be variously disagreeable and ingeniously unclean in the station in which it has pleased God to place her.

Humanitarian. A person who believes the Saviour was human and himself is divine.

Husband. One who, having dined, is charged with the care of the plate.

Hypocrite. One who, professing virtues that he does not respect, secures the advantage of seeming to be what he despises.

I. This is the first letter of the alphabet, the first word of the language, the first thought of the mind, the first object of affection. The frank yet graceful use of '*I*' distinguishes a good writer from a bad; the latter carries with it the manner of a thief trying to cloak his loot.

Idiot. A member of a large and powerful tribe whose influence in human affairs has always been dominant and controlling. The Idiot's activity is not confined to any special field or thought or action, but 'pervades and regulates the whole'. He has the last word in everything; his decision is unappealable.

He sets the fashions of opinion and taste, dictates the limitations of speech and circumscribes conduct with a deadline.

Ignoramus. A person unacquainted with certain kinds of knowledge familiar to yourself, and having certain other kinds that you know nothing about.

Immigrant. An unenlightened person who thinks one country better than another.

Immoral. Inexpedient. Whatever in the long run and with regard to the greater number of instances men find to be generally inexpedient comes to be considered wrong, wicked, immoral.

Impartial. Unable to perceive any promise of personal advantage from espousing either side of a controversy or adopting either of two conflicting opinions.

Impeccable. Not liable to detection.

Implacable. Not to be appeased without a large sum of money.

Impostor. A rival aspirant to public honours.

Impropriety. Next to vulgarity, the highest conceivable degree of sin.

Impunity. Wealth.

Incompatability. In matrimony a similarity of tastes, particularly the taste for domination.

Indecision. The chief element of success; 'for whereas,' saith Sir Thomas Brewbold, 'there is but one way to do nothing and divers ways to do something, whereof to a surety, only one is the right way, it followeth that he who from indecision standeth still hath not so many chances of going astray as he who pusheth forwards' – a most clear and satisfactory exposition of the matter.

Inexpedient. Not calculated to advance one's interests.

Ingratitude. A form of self-respect that is not inconsistent with acceptance of favours.

Inhumanity. One of the characteristic qualities of humanity.

Innocence. The state or condition of a criminal whose counsel has fixed the jury.

Insane. Addicted to the conviction that others are insane.

Inventor. A person who makes an ingenious arrangement of wheels, levers and springs, and believes it civilization.

Jealousy. The seamy side of love.

Joy. An emotion variously excited, but in its highest degree arising from the contemplation of grief in another.

Judge. A person who is always interfering in disputes in which he has no personal interest.

Jury. A number of persons appointed by a court to assist the attorney in preventing Law from degenerating into Justice.

Kiss. A word invented by the poets as a rhyme for 'bliss'. It is supposed to signify, in a general way, some kind of rite or ceremony appertaining to a good understanding; but the manner of its performance is unknown to this lexicographer.

Labour. One of the processes by which A acquires property for B.

Land. A part of the earth's surface, considered as property. The theory that land is property subject to private ownership and control is the foundation of modern society, and is eminently worthy of the superstructure. Carried to its logical conclusion, it means that some have the right to prevent others from living; for the right to own implies the right exclusively to occupy; and in fact laws of trespass are enacted wherever property in land is recognized. It follows that if the whole area of terra firma is owned by A, B and C, there will be no place for D, E, F and G to be born, or, as trespassers, to exist.

Laughter. An interior convulsion, producing a distortion of the features and accompanied by inarticulate noises. It is infectious and, though intermittent, incurable.

Lawyer. One skilled in circumvention of the law.

Laziness. Unwarranted repose of manner in a person of low degree.

League. A union of two or more parties, factions or associations for promoting some purpose, commonly nefarious.

Learning. The kind of ignorance affected by (and affecting) civilized races, as distinguished from ignorance, the sort of learning incurred by savages.

Leisure. Lucid intervals in a disordered life.

Liberty. One of Imagination's most precious possessions.

Life. A spiritual pickle preserving the body from decay. We live in daily apprehension of its loss; yet when lost it is not missed. The question, 'Is life worth living?' has been much discussed; particularly by those who think it is not, many of whom have written at great length in support of their view and by careful observance of the laws of health enjoyed for long terms of years the honours of successful controversy.

Literally. Figuratively. As, 'the pond was literally full of fish' and 'the ground was literally alive with snakes'.

Liver. A large red organ thoughtfully provided by nature to be bilious with.

Logic. The art of thinking and reasoning in strict accordance with the limitations of the human misunderstanding.

Longevity. Uncommon extension of the fear of death.

Loquacity. A disorder which renders the sufferer unable to curb his tongue when you wish to talk.

Love. The folly of thinking much of another before one knows anything of oneself. A temporary insanity curable by marriages or by removal of the patient from the influences under which he incurred the disorder. This disease, like caries and many other ailments, is prevalent among civilized races living under artificial conditions; barbarous nations breathing pure air and eating simple food enjoy immunity from its ravages. It is sometimes fatal, but more frequently to the physician than to the patient.

Machination. The method employed by one's opponents in baffling one's open and honourable efforts to do the right thing.

Mad. Affected with a high degree of intellectual independence; not conforming to standards of thought, speech and action derived by the conformants from study of themselves; at odds with the majority; in short, unusual. It is noteworthy that persons are pronounced mad by officials destitute of evidence that they themselves are sane.

Male. A member of the unconsidered, or negligible sex. The male of the human race is commonly known (to the female) as Mere Man. The genus has two varieties: *good providers* and *bad providers.*

Mammon. The god of the world's leading religion. His chief temple is in the holy city of New York.

Man. An animal so lost in rapturous contemplation of what he thinks he is as to overlook what he indubitably ought to be. His chief occupation is extermination of other animals and his own species, which, however, multiplies with such insistent rapidity as to infest the whole habitable earth and Canada.

Marriage. The state or condition of a community consisting of a master, a mistress and two slaves, making in all, two.

Marvellous. Not understood.

Mediate. To butt in.

Meekness. Uncommon patience in planning a revenge that is worthwhile.

Minor. Less objectionable.

Miracle. An act or event out of the order of nature and unaccountable as beating a normal hand of four kings and an ace with four aces and a king.

Misdemeanour. An infraction of the law having less dignity than a felony and constituting no claim to admittance into the best criminal society.

Miss. A title with which we brand unmarried women to indicate that they are in the market. Miss, Missis (Mrs) and Mister (Mr) are the three most distinctly disagreeable words in the language, in sound and sense. Two are corruptions of Mistress, the other of Master. In the general abolition of social titles in this our country they miraculously escaped to plague us. If we must have them let us be consistent and give one to the unmarried man. I venture to suggest Mush, abbreviated to Mh.

Mortality. The part of immortality that we know about.

Mythology. The body of a primitive people's beliefs concerning its origin, early history, heroes, deities and so forth, as distinguished from the true accounts which it invents later.

Novel. A short story padded.

Nudity. That quality in art which is most painful to the prurient.

Obsolete. No longer used by the timid. Said chiefly of words. A word which some lexicógrapher has marked obsolete is ever thereafter an object of dread and loathing to the fool writer, but if it is a good word and has no exact modern equivalent equally good, it is good enough for the good writer. Indeed, a writer's attitude to 'obsolete' words is as true a measure of his literary ability as anything except the character of his work. A dictionary of obsolete and obsolescent words would not only be singularly rich in strong and sweet parts of speech; it would add large possessions to the vocabulary of every competent writer who might not happen to be a competent reader.

Old. In that stage of usefulness which is not inconsistent with general inefficiency; as, an old man. Discredited by lapse of time and offensive to the popular taste; as, an old book.

Omen. A sign that something will happen if nothing happens.

Once. Enough.

Opportunity. A favourable occasion for grasping a disappointment.

Opposition. In politics the party that prevents the government from running amuck by hamstringing it.

Optimism. The doctrine, or belief, that everything is beautiful, including what is ugly; everything good, especially the bad; and everything right that is wrong. Being a blind faith, it is inaccessible to the light of disproof – an intellectual disorder, yielding to no treatment but death. It is hereditary, but fortunately not contagious.

Optimist. A proponent of the doctrine that black is white.

Overwork. A dangerous disorder affecting high public functionaries who want to go fishing.

Pagan. A benighted person who prefers home-made deities and indigenous religious rites.

Pain. An uncomfortable frame of mind that may have a physical basis in something that is being done to the body, or may be purely mental, caused by the good fortune of another.

Pardon. To remit a penalty and restore to a life of crime. To add to the lure of crime the temptation of ingratitude.

Partisan. An adherent without sense.

Passport. A document treacherously inflicted upon a citizen going abroad, exposing him as an alien and pointing him out for special reprobation and outrage.

Patience. A minor form of despair, disguised as a virtue.

Peace. In international affairs, a period of cheating between two periods of fighting.

Perseverance. A lowly virtue whereby mediocrity achieves an inglorious success.

Pessimism. A philosophy forced upon the convictions of the observer by the disheartening prevalence of the optimist with his scarecrow hope and his unsightly smile.

Philosophy. A route of many roads leading from nowhere to nothing.

Piano. A parlour utensil for subduing the impenitent visitor. It is operated by depressing the keys of the machine and the spirits of the audience.

Picture. A representation in two dimensions of something wearisome in three.

Pitiful. The state of an enemy or opponent after an imaginary encounter with oneself.

Plagiarize. To take the thought or style of another writer whom one has never, never read.

Plan. To bother about the best method of accomplishing an accidental result.

Pleasure. An emotion engendered by something advantageous to one's self or disastrous to others. In the plural this word signifies those mostly artificial aids to melancholy that deepen the general gloom of existence with a particular dejection.

Plunder. To take the property of another without observing the decent and customary reticences of theft.

Politeness. The most acceptable hypocrisy.

Politics. A means of livelihood affected by the more degraded portion of our criminal classes. A strife of interests masquerading as a contest of principles. The conduct of public affairs for private advantages.

Polygamy. Too much of a good thing.

Positive. Mistaken at the top of one's voice.

Pray. To ask that the laws of the universe be annulled in behalf of a single petitioner confessedly unworthy.

Precocious. Describing a four-year-old who elopes with his sister's doll.

Preference. A sentiment or frame of mind, induced by the erroneous belief that one thing is better than another.

Prejudice. A vagrant opinion without visible means of support.

Prescription. A physician's guess at what will best prolong the situation with least harm to the patient.

Press. A mighty magnifying machine which, by the aid of 'we' and printer's ink, changes the squeak of a mouse into the roar of an editorial lion, on whose utterances the nation (presumably) hangs with bated breath.

Prevaricate. To say that 'she has expressive eyes' when a friend asks you if you think his girl is handsome.

Primitive. People who believe that 'honesty is the best policy'.

Prodigal. A young man who used to go to the dogs, but now generally goes straight to the devil.

Property. The distinction between a whisky-drinking tramp and a champagne-guzzling millionaire.

Prophetic. Dreaming about the devil the night before you are married.

Provincial. Peculiar.

Prudent. A man who believes ten per cent of what he hears, a quarter of what he reads, and half of what he sees.

Public. An undefined number of private persons.

Punishment. A weapon which Justice has almost forgotten how to use.

Puritan. A pious gentleman who believed in letting all people do as-he-liked.

Quantity. A good substitute for quality when you are hungry.

Quotation. The act of repeating erroneously the words of another. The words erroneously repeated.

Rash. Insensible to the value of our advice.

Rational. Devoid of all delusions save those of observation, experience and reflection.

Really. Apparently.

Reconciliation. A suspension of hostilities. An armed truce for the purpose of digging up the dead.

Referendum. A law for submission of proposed legislation to a popular vote to learn the nonsense of public opinion.

Refreshing. Meeting a man who believes all he reads in the papers.

Relations. People that you call on, or that call on you, according to whether they are rich or poor.

Renown. A degree of distinction between notoriety and fame – a little more supportable than the one and a little more intolerable than the other. Sometimes it is conferred by an unfriendly and inconsiderate hand.

Representative. A gentleman who looks after the interests of his constituents – when they don't conflict with his own.

Reprobate. A venerable old gent who 'would if he could'.

Republic. A form of government in which equal justice is administered to all who can afford to pay for it.

Resident. Unable to leave.

Resign. A good thing to do when you are going to be kicked out.

Resolute. Obstinate in a course that we approve.

Responsibility. A detachable burden easily shifted to the shoulders of God, Fate, Fortune, Luck or one's neighbour.

Revenge. Sending your girl's love letters to your rival after he has married her.

Revolution. In politics, an abrupt change in the form of misgovernment.

Rich. Holding in trust and subject to an accounting the property of the indolent, the incompetent, the unthrifty, the envious and the luckless. That is the view that prevails in the underworld, where the Brotherhood of Man finds its most logical development and candid advocacy. To denizens of the midworld the word means good and wise.

Riddle. Who elects our rulers?

Riot. A popular entertainment given to the military by innocent bystanders.

Road. A strip of land along which one may pass from where it is too tiresome to be to where it is futile to go.

Robber. A vulgar name for one who is successful in obtaining the property of others.

Rural. Mud, hogs and badly-cooked food.

Saint. A dead sinner revised and edited.

Scribbler. A professional writer whose views are antagonistic to one's own.

Self-evident. Evident to one's self and nobody else.

Selfish. Devoid of consideration for the selfishness of others.

Success. The one unpardonable sin against one's fellows.

Take. To acquire, frequently by force but preferably by stealth.

Technicality. In an English court a man named Home was tried for slander in having accused a neighbour of murder. His exact words were : 'Sir Thomas Holt hath taken a cleaver and stricken his cook upon the head, so that one side of the head fell upon one shoulder and the other side upon the other shoulder.' The defendant was acquitted by instruction of the court, the learned judges holding that the words did not charge murder, for they did not affirm the death of the cook, that being only an inference.

Telephone. An invention of the devil which abrogates some of the advantages of making a disagreeable person keep his distance.

Truth. An ingenious compound of desirability and appearance. Discovery of truth is the sole purpose of philosophy, which is the most ancient occupation of the human mind and has a fair prospect of existing with increasing activity to the end of time.

Truthful. Dumb and illiterate.

Ultimatum. In diplomacy, a last demand before resorting to concessions.

Un-American. Wicked, intolerable, heathenish.

Urbanity. The kind of civility that urban observers ascribe to dwellers in all cities but New York. Its commonest expression is heard in the words, 'I beg your pardon'. It is not inconsistent with disregard of the rights of others.

Valour. A soldierly compound of vanity, duty and the gambler's hope.

Virtues. Certain abstentions.

Vote. The instrument and symbol of a freeman's power to make a fool of himself and a wreck of his country.

Weather. A permanent topic of conversation among persons whom it does not interest, but who have inherited the tendency to chatter about it from naked arboreal ancestors whom it keenly concerned.

Wedding. A ceremony at which two persons undertake to become one, one undertakes to become nothing, and nothing undertakes to become supportable.

Woman. An animal usually living in the vicinity of Man, and having a rudimentary susceptibility to domestication.

Wrath. Anger of a superior quality and degree, appropriate to exalted characters and momentous occasions.

Year. A period of 365 disappointments.

Zeal. A certain nervous disorder afflicting the young and inexperienced.

Ambrose Bierce's definition of 'perseverance' is one of my favourites: 'A lowly virtue whereby mediocrity achieves an inglorious success.'

It could certainly be said to apply to at least one of Britain's more recent Prime Ministers! That's one of the joys of Bierce: almost everything he wrote is apt today. However, even ardent canoozers of his wit (as my grandfather would have described Bierce connoisseurs) have to admit that there are some contemporary eventualities that Bierce seems not to have anticipated back at the turn of the century. To survive in the 1980s you have to realize that not everyone means what they say: so to help you get by till 1984 (and if there ever was a portrait painted of Hell George Orwell achieved it in his novel), I have been bold enough to produce some 'diabolical definitions' for the modern world. They're not perhaps in the same league as those of the Master, but I hope they will still raise the occasional smile and the odd nod of recognition.

. . . TO ROSSITER

Absolutely. Probably.

Abundance. Enough for me.

Acupuncture. An unorthodox treatment for various diseases that needles orthodox medical practitioners.

Administrator. One who shuffles paper, generally achieving little or nothing of consequence.

Air. A gaseous cesspit for the dumping of various poisons.

Alien. Not British.

Apollo. The name given to a lunatic scheme for transporting a small number of Americans from the Earth to the Earth's only natural satellite.

Assassin. Murderer.

Blood. A red liquid material often found in the alcohol streams of certain individuals.

Bomb. An argument used by temporary maniacs.

Bridge. A way for two couples to pass their time together when none of them has anything to say to the others.

Business. Organized cheating.

Chastity. A rare condition affecting a few hapless souls. Nowadays, fortunately, it is easily curable.

Cigarette. A foul invention emitting all manner of noxious substances. It is designed to annoy those who do not use it, and to kill those who do. The latter enjoy it more than the former.

Common Sense. Un-common sense. Especially rare in *Homo sap.*

Company Perks. Fiddles arranged with the taxman.

Comprehensive School. A large-scale plant for the systematic production of consistent mediocrity.

Computer. A modern device for spewing out great quantities of scrap paper and incorrect information. Currently, second only to Mammon in the worship stakes.

Concorde. A hideously expensive airborne contraption for getting from A to B, that befuddles the senses of the traveller even more quickly than other, more mundane, airborne devices.

Cordon Bleu. A term used to describe an individual who is particularly adept at disguising food.

Criminal. One who gets caught.

Decimalization. A sort of bonus inflation.

Devolution. A form of late 20th-century Celtic lunacy.

Dieting. Eating sensibly.

Discotheque. A very popular and modern place of entertainment, bearing certain similarities to Hades.

Driving Test. An examination for the purpose of issuing licences to idiots to go forth and cause mayhem.

Economy. A complicated system involving bankruptcies, loans, overdrafts, and the like.

Education. Originally intended for imparting the three R's. The number now imparted has fallen to zero.

Enthusiasm. Naive keenness, curable by small doses of experience.

Environment. Man's surroundings. A term only recently discovered, which is strange given Man's antiquity.

Estate Agent. One of a proliferating band of scoundrels who extract vast sums of money for insubstantial amounts of work.

Fashion. That which is unwearable until everyone else is wearing it, by which time it is unfashionable.

First Class Post. The superior method of having one's letters delayed, as distinguished from 'second class post', the latter being the inferior method.

Football Fan. One whose goal is trouble.

Friends. People whose numbers multiply when you are doing well.

Go-slow. Chaos.

Health Service. A system of providing health care to the population. Paradoxically, the Health Service has been in poor health ever since its birth.

Heathrow. A vast desert through which many travellers are forced to journey when travelling to and from foreign parts.

Hobby. A device for promoting dejection and boredom. A gentle exercise for intellectual debility.

Honesty. Not getting found out.

Honeymoon. The beginning of a downhill slide.

Honourable. Dishonourable. As, 'the honourable gentleman is a scurvy cur'.

House of Lords. A body of elderly persons charged with high duties and misdemeanours.

Incest. Relations with one's relations.

Interregnum. A grand-sounding name for nothing more than a gap, wherein nothing actually happens.

Juggernaut. A vast contraption designed to emit foul stenches, create harsh roars, and disturb pleasant byways. Another of civilization's wonders.

Manifesto. Organized gibberish masquerading as a panacea for all Society's ills.

Manners. Obsolete affectations. Those small rituals whereby one demonstrated one's politeness to one's fellow creatures.

Member of Parliament. A harmless drudge.

Mime. A dramatic device which does little violence to the language.

Mini. A cheap and uncomfortable way of traversing the route between A and B, but socially acceptable.

Nostalgia. Fond thoughts of imaginary times gone past.

Nuclear Missile. An agency reserved for use by the most civilized nations for the settlement of disputes that might become troublesome if left unadjusted. Unfortunately, too many formerly uncivilized nations are becoming civilized.

Persuasion. Arm twisting.

Philanthropist. A rich person who enjoys having his pocket picked.

Pollution. The chief product and authenticating sign of civilization.

Pornography. That which excites, whether from approval or disapproval.

Psychiatrist. A person who studies the problems of others in an attempt to understand his own problems.

Public Opinion Poll. A crude device not dissimilar to a weather-vane.

Public School. A training ground for dunces.

Rates. A legitimate protection racket organized by local politicians.

Rationalize. To cut. As 'British Rail is going to rationalize a number of its rural services'.

Record Player. An irritating toy that restores life to dead noises.

Robbery. Redistribution of wealth.

Rolls Royce. An expensive and luxurious way of traversing the route from A to B, but socially frowned upon.

Scarcity. Not enough for me.

Sea. A liquid cesspit for the dumping of various poisons.

Skin. That which keeps the human form in the human form.

Slang. Language which rolls up its sleeves, spits on its hands, and gets down to work. Disparaged by some, but used by all.

Television. An advanced technical method of stopping people from making their own entertainments.

Tourist. A foreigner who is not where he belongs.

Virginity. An affliction similar to chastity (q.v.).

Vodka. A pagan spirit, much worshipped in Britain of late.

Wealth Tax. Capital punishment.

Work-to-rule. Chaos.

THE DEVIL'S LAWS

FROM MURPHY TO ROSSITER

I didn't get where I am today without realizing that every day you learn something new. For example, since getting up this morning I have discovered two Fundamental Laws:

1 If you consecrate a day to quietly working on your edition of *The Devil's Bedside Book* inevitably that will be the day the central heating pipes choose to burst and fill your home with lukewarm water.

2 If a plumber is coming to attend to your collapsed central heating system and he leaves his tools in the graveyard at the back of your house, inevitably when he returns from his teabreak the tools will have been buried beneath a coffin. (You don't believe it, do you? But it's true, I promise.)

'Reginald Perrin' and 'C.J.' – those immortal characters created by David Nobbs who were played respectively by me and John Barron in the three *Perrin* series on television – could well have benefited from this chapter, because it features those Laws which, while they may not quite come into the Isaac Newton/Albert Einstein class, are of indisputable value when it comes to coping with modern life. Many of these Laws have already achieved 'classic' status, but some are still comparatively unknown. These are Rossiter's Laws; and my hope is that they will soon stand with those of the masters – Murphy's Law and Parkinson's Law.

Agnes Allen's Law
Almost anything is easier to get into than out of.

The Air Travel Law
When the aeroplane you are on is late, the aeroplane that you want to transfer to is on time or early.

Allison's Precept
The most straightforward method of testing someone's expertise in a particular area is the ability to win money in a series of bets on future occurrences in that area.

Law of Annoyance
If you put away a tool that you're certain you've finished with, you will need it again instantly.

Anthony's Workshop Law
Any tool, when dropped, always rolls into the least accessible corner of the workshop. (There is a corollary to this: on the way to the corner, any dropped tool will first always strike your toes.)

The Army's First Law
If it moves, salute it. If it doesn't move, pick it up. And if you can't pick it up, paint it.

The Army's Second Law
Any order that can be misunderstood will be.

The Army's Third Law
All orders are capable of being misunderstood.

Atwood's Book Law
No books are lost by lending except those you particularly want to keep.

Barth's Division
There are two types of people: those who divide people into two types, and those who don't.

Beauregard's Law
When you're up to your nose, keep your mouth shut.

Beckhap's Law
Beauty multiplied by brains equals a constant.

Beifeld's Principle
The probability of a young man meeting a desirable receptive

young female increases by pyramidal progression when he is already in the company of (i) a date, (ii) his wife and (iii) a better-looking and richer male friend.

First Law of Bicycling
No matter which way you go, it's uphill and against the wind.

Second Law of Bicycling
The likelihood of rain is in direct proportion to your desire to use your bicycle.

Blaauw's Law
Established technology persists in spite of new technology.

Boling's Postulate
If you're feeling fine, don't worry. You'll get over it.

Boren's First Law
When in doubt, mumble.

Boren's Second Law
When in trouble, delegate.

Boren's Third Law
When in charge, ponder.

Borkowski's Law
You can't guard against the arbitrary.

Boyle's Law for the Expert
If not controlled, work will flow to the competent man until he submerges.

First Law of Bridge
It's always your partner's fault.

Second Law of Bridge
If it wasn't your partner's fault, your opponents were damned lucky.

Brien's Law
At some time in the life of every organization, its ability to succeed in spite of itself runs out.

Broder's Law
Anybody who wants to be President so much that he'll spend two years organizing and campaigning for it is not to be trusted with the office.

Bromiley's Maxim
What's not worth doing is not worth doing well.

Brooke's Law
Whenever a system becomes completely defined, some damned fool discovers something which either abolishes the system or expands it beyond recognition.

Bucy's Law
Nothing is ever accomplished by being reasonable.

Bunuel's Law
Overdoing things is always harmful. This applies particularly to efficiency.

Canada Bill Jones' Motto
It's morally wrong to allow suckers to keep their money.

Captain Penny's Law
You can fool all of the people some of the time, and some of the people all of the time. But you can't fool your mother.

Chamberlain's First Law
The big guys always win.

Chamberlain's Second Law
Everything tastes more or less like chicken.

Cheops' Pyramid Law
Nothing ever gets built on schedule or within its budget.

Chisholm's Law
When things just can't get any worse, they will.

The First Law of Christmas Presents
If it doesn't need a plug, batteries are never included.

The Second Law of Christmas Presents
It it doesn't need batteries, a plug is never included.

The Third Law of Christmas Presents
Everything is constructed to break on 26 December.

The Fourth Law of Christmas Presents
If you can wear it, it'll be the wrong size.

The Fifth Law of Christmas Presents
The colour is never right.

The Sixth Law of Christmas Presents
Santa Claus is an incorrigible practical joker.

Churchill's Commentary on Man
Man will occasionally stumble over the truth, but most of the time he will pick himself up and continue on.

Clarke's First Law
When a distinguished but elderly scientist states that something is possible, he is almost certainly right. When he states that something is impossible, he is very probably wrong.

Clarke's Second Law
The only way to discover the limits of the possible is to go beyond them into the impossible.

Clarke's Third Law
Any sufficiently advanced technology is indistinguishable from magic.

Clarke's Law of Revolutionary Ideas
Every revolutionary idea evokes three stages of reaction. They may be summed up by the three phrases:

1 'It's impossible – don't waste my time.'
2 'It's possible, but isn't worth doing.'
3 'I said it was a good idea all along.'

Cohen's Law
What really matters is the name you succeed in imposing on the facts – not the facts themselves.

Cole's Axiom
The sum of the intelligence on the planet is constant. The population is growing.

Colonel Stapp's Ironical Paradox
The universal aptitude for ineptitude makes any human accomplishment an incredible miracle.

The Law of Committee Dynamics
The less you enjoy serving on committees, the more likely you are to be pressed to do so.

Commoner's Second Law of Ecology
Nothing ever goes away.

The Law of Communication
In any organization, if communication is improved between different levels in that organization, the inevitable result is a greatly increased area for misunderstanding.

The First Law of Computing
To err is human, but to really foul things up requires a computer.

The Second Law of Computing
If it looks wrong, it is wrong. If it looks as if it might be right, the chances are it's still wrong.

Coolidge's Observation
When more and more people are thrown out of work, unemployment results.

Cooper's Law
If you don't understand a particular word in a piece of technical writing, just ignore it. The piece will make perfect sense without it.

Cooper's Meta-law
A proliferation of new laws creates a proliferation of new loopholes.

Cornuelle's Law
Authority tends to assign jobs to those least able to do them.

Cripps' Law
When travelling with children on one's holidays, at least one child of any number of children will want to go to the toilet exactly halfway between any two given toilets.

Dave's Rule of Street Survival
Speak softly, and own a big mean Doberman Pinscher.

First Law of Debate
Never argue with a fool – people might not know the difference.

Dieter's Law
Food that tastes best has the highest number of calories.

Dirksen's Three Laws of Politics

1 Get elected.
2 Get re-elected.
3 Don't get mad; get even.

Donohue's Law
If a thing's worth doing, make sure you do it for money.

Dow's Law
In any hierarchical organization, the higher the level, the greater the confusion.

Eddington's Theory
The number of different hypotheses needed to explain a given scientific phenomenon is inversely proportional to the knowledge available.

Ehrman's Commentaries

1. Things will get worse before they get better.
2. Who said things would get better?

Epstein's Law
If you think the problem is bad now, just wait until we've solved it.

Etorre's Observation
In a bank, supermarket, traffic jam, or whatever, the other queue always, always moves faster.

Everitt's Second Law of Thermodynamics
Confusion is always increasing in society. Only if someone or something works very hard can this confusion be reduced to order in a limited area. Even then, this effort will still result in an increase in confusion of society at large.

The Experimenter's Data Law
In any collection of data, the figures that are obviously correct, beyond all need of checking, are the ones that contain the errors.

The Experimenter's Law of Animal Behaviour
Any well-trained experimental animal in a controlled environment and subject to a controlled stimulation will do as it damned well pleases.

Fetridge's Law
Important things that are supposed to happen do not happen, especially when people are looking. Conversely, things that

are supposed not to happen do happen, especially when people are looking.

Fett's Law
It's usually impossible to repeat a successful experiment.

Finagle's Rules

1 To study a subject best, make sure you understand it thoroughly before you start.
2 Whatever you do or don't do, write something down – it indicates you've been working.
3 In case of doubt, make it sound convincing.
4 Do not believe in miracles — rely on them.

Finagle's First Law
If it works, then something must be wrong.

Finagle's Second Law
No matter what the anticipated result of any experiment or trial, there will always be someone eager to:

1 misinterpret it;
2 fake it; or
3 believe it happened to his own pet theory.

Finagle's Third Law
If you've got a problem, no-one that you ask for help will be able to help. Everyone who stops by with unsought advice will solve it immediately.

Finagle's Fourth Law
Once something is fouled up, anything done to improve it can only make it worse.

FitzGibbon's Law
Creativity varies inversely with the number of cooks involved with the broth.

Fowler's Observation
The only imperfect thing in Nature is the human race.

Franklin's Law
Blessed is he who expects nothing, for he shall not be disappointed.

Freeman's Commentary on Ginsberg's Theorem
Every major philosophy that attempts to make life seem meaningful is based on the negation of one part of Ginsberg's Theorem. For example:

1 Capitalism is based on the assumption that you can win.
2 Socialism is based on the assumption that you can break even.
3 Mysticism is based on the assumption that you can quit the game.

Galbraith's Law of Political Wisdom
Anyone who says four times he isn't going to resign definitely will.

The First Law of Gardening
The rake you step on is always teeth up, so that it not only injures your foot but smacks you in the mouth with its handle.

The Second Law of Gardening
Other people's tools work only in other people's gardens.

The Third Law of Gardening
Gimmicky devices don't work.

The Fourth Law of Gardening
You get the most flowers or vegetables of the sort that you need the least.

The Fifth Law of Gardening
It always rains after you've watered the lawn.

The Sixth Law of Gardening
If you've spent days planning to have a bonfire, when you finally light it all your neighbours decide to hang out their washing.

Getty's Reminder
The meek shall inherit the earth, but *not* its mineral rights.

Gilb's First Law of Unreliability
Computers are unreliable, but human beings are even more so.

Gilb's Second Law of Unreliability
Anything which depends on human reliability is unreliable.

Gilb's Third Law of Unreliability
Undetectable errors are infinite in variety, in contrast to detectable errors, which, by definition, are limited.

Ginsberg's Theorem

1 You can't win.
2 You can't break even.
3 You can't even quit the game.

Ginsberg's Theorem's Follow-on
What are the rules of the game, anyway?

Glatum's Law
The perceived usefulness of any article is inversely proportional to its actual usefulness once bought and paid for.

Golden Rule of Arts and Sciences
Whoever has the gold makes the rules.

The Rule of Great People
Whenever somebody you greatly admire and respect appears to be thinking deep thoughts, they are probably thinking about lunch.

Gresham's Law
Trivial matters are handled promptly. Important matters are never solved.

Gummidge's Law
The amount of expertise varies in inverse proportion to the number of statements understood by the general public.

Gumperson's Law
The probability of anything happening is in inverse ratio to its desirability. Thus: vacant parking spaces are always on the other side of the street; you can throw an extinguished cigarette end out of a car window and start a raging forest fire, whereas it will take an hour to get a blaze going in a fireplace loaded with dry wood and sloshed with paraffin.

Haldane's Law
The universe is not only queerer than we imagine, it's queerer than we can imagine.

Hartley's Law
You can lead a horse to water, but if you can get him to float on his back, then you've really got something.

Heller's Law
The first myth of management is that it exists.

Heller's Other Law
Nobody really knows what's going on anywhere in the organization.

Hendrickson's Law
If a problem causes many meetings, the meetings eventually become more important than the problem.

Herblock's Law
If it's good, they'll stop making it.

Hoare's Law of Large Problems
Inside every large problem is a small problem struggling to get out.

Horner's Postulate
Experience varies directly with the amount of equipment ruined.

Howe's Law
Everyone has a scheme that won't work.

Hull's Warning
Never insult an alligator until after you have crossed the river.

IBM's Pollyanna Principle
Machines should work; people should think.

The Iceberg Theorem
Eight-ninths of everything is invisible.

Iles' Law
There's always an easier way to do it. When looking directly at the easier way, especially for long periods, you will not see it.

Law of the Individual
Nobody really cares or understands what anyone else is doing.

Law of Institutions
The opulence of the decorations in the front office varies inversely with the fundamental solvency of the firm.

Iron Law of Distribution
Them that has, gets.

Issawi's Law
The total amount of evil in any system remains constant: hence, any diminution in one direction is accompanied by an increase in another. For example, a reduction in unemployment is accompanied by increased air pollution.

Issawi's Observation
Each system has its own way of consuming vast amounts of paper: in socialist societies, by completing large forms in quadruplicate; in capitalist societies, by putting up huge posters and wrapping every article in four layers of cardboard.

Jacquin's Postulate on Democratic Government
No man's life, liberty or property are safe while the legislature is in session.

Jay's Law of Leadership
Changing things is central to leadership, and changing them before anyone else is creativity.

Jenkinson's Law
It won't work.

John's Collateral Corollary
In order to get a loan, you must first prove you don't need it.

Johnson's First Law
When any mechanical or electrical contrivance fails, it will do so at the most inconvenient possible time.

Johnson's Second Law
If, in a given month, only three worthwhile social events take place, they will all fall on the same evening.

Johnson's Third Law
If you miss one issue of a magazine, it will be the issue which contained the article you were most anxious to read.

Johnson and Laird's Law
Toothache tends to start on Saturday evening, immediately the dentist has closed.

Jones' Law
The man who can smile when things go wrong has thought of someone he can blame it on.

Jones' Motto
Friends come and go, but enemies accumulate.

Juhani's Law
The compromise will always be more expensive than either of the suggestions it is compromising.

Katz's Law
Men and nations will act rationally when all other possibilities have been exhausted.

Kerr-Martin's Law

1 In dealing with their own problems, university lecturers are the most extreme conservatives.
2 In dealing with other people's problems, they are the most extreme liberals.

Kitman's Law
Pure drivel tends to drive off the television screen plain ordinary drivel.

Klipstein's First Law
If a research worker makes a patent application, it will be preceded by one week by a similar application made by a totally independent research worker.

Klipstein's Second Law
Firmness of delivery dates is inversely proportional to the tightness of the schedule.

Klipstein's Third Law
Any wire cut to length will be too short.

Klipstein's Fourth Law
If an object is made up of a certain number of components (say, n), then there will never be more than $(n - 1)$ components in stock.

Klipstein's Fifth Law
An electrical circuit designed to protect itself when the power fails will invariably end up destroying other circuits.

Klipstein's Sixth Law
Failures do not appear until after the final inspection.

Levy's Third Law
That segment of the community with which one has the greatest sympathy as a liberal inevitably turns out to be the most narrow-minded and bigoted segment of the community.

Levy's Eighth Law
No amount of genius can overcome a preoccupation with detail.

Levy's Ninth Law
Only God can make a random selection.

Lewis' Law
No matter how long or how hard you shop for an item, after you've bought it it will be on sale somewhere cheaper.

Lord Falkland's Rule
When it is not necessary to make a decision, it is not necessary to make a decision.

Lowery's Law
If it jams, force it. If it breaks, it needed replacing anyway.

Maier's Law
If the facts do not conform to the theory, they must be disposed of. (This has a corollary: the bigger the theory the better.)

Malek's Law
Any simple idea will be worded in the most complicated way.

Management Truths

1. Think before you act; it's not your money.
2. All good management is the expression of one great idea.
3. No executive devotes effort to proving himself wrong.
4. If sophisticated calculations are needed to justify an action, don't do it.

Match's Maxim
A fool in a high station is like a man on top of a high mountain; everything appears small to him and he appears small to everybody.

Matsch's Law
It's better to have a horrible ending than to have horrors without end.

McClaughry's Codicil to Jones' Motto
To make an enemy, do someone a favour.

McNaughton's Rule
Any argument worth making within a bureaucracy must be capable of being expressed in a simple declarative sentence that is obviously true once stated.

Mencken's Law
Those who can – do.
Those who cannot – teach.
Those who cannot teach – administrate.

Miksch's Law
If a string has one end, then it has another end.

Miller's Law
You can't tell how deep a puddle is until you step in it.

Murphy's Law, its Corollaries, and Revisions of it
Stated in its simplest form, Murphy's Law is this:

> If anything can go wrong, it will.

As with most laws, this has several corollaries, or consequences. There are at least eleven corollaries currently known, but there are doubtless others waiting to be unearthed.

The eleven corollaries:

1. Nothing is as easy as it looks.
2. Everything takes longer than you think.
3. If there is a possibility of several things going wrong, the one to go wrong will be the one that will cause the most damage.
4. If you perceive that there are four possible ways in which something can go wrong, and circumvent these, then a fifth way will promptly appear.
5. Left to themselves, things always go from bad to worse.
6. Whenever you set out to do something, you always find that something else has to be done first.

7 Every solution breeds new problems.
8 It is impossible to make anything foolproof because fools are ingenious.
9 If everything seems to be going well, you have obviously overlooked something.
10 Nature always sides with the hidden flaw.
11 Mother Nature is a bitch.

Murphy also discovered a law describing the economic consequences of his main Law. Stated simply, this is:

> When something goes wrong, matter is always damaged in direct proportion to its value.

After much research into the underlying physical causes of his Law, Murphy issued his Revised Law. At first sight this appears to be rather sweeping, but nevertheless, observation demonstrates it to be true. Murphy's Revised Law is:

> When anything goes wrong, everything goes wrong all at once.

One of Murphy's co-researchers was an Irishman named O'Toole. O'Toole's most profound Observation on the ways of the universe can best be summed up as follows.

> Murphy was an optimist.

Murphy's Law of Research
Enough research will always tend to support your theory.

Murphy's Philosophy
Smile . . . tomorrow will be worse.

Newton's Unknown Law
A bird in the hand is safer than one overhead.

The Ninety-Ninety Rule
The first ninety per cent of any task takes ninety per cent of the time.

The last ten per cent of the task takes another ninety per cent of the time.

Non-reciprocal Expectation Laws
Negative expectations yield negative results.
Positive expectations yield negative results.

Law of Observation
Nothing looks as good close up as it does from far away.

Law of Observation Restated
Nothing looks as good from far away as it does close up.

Oeser's Law
There is a tendency for the person in the most powerful position in any organization to spend all of his or her time serving on committees and signing letters.

Old and Kahn's Law
The efficiency of a committee meeting is inversely proportional to the number of participants and the time spent on deliberations.

The Ordering Principle
The supplies necessary for yesterday's experiment must be ordered no later than 5.00 p.m. tomorrow evening.

Pardo's First Postulate
Anything good in life is either illegal, immoral or fattening.

Pardo's Second Postulate
The three faithful things in life are money, a dog and an old woman.

Pardo's Third Postulate
Don't care if you're rich or not, as long as you can live comfortably and have everything you want.

Parker's Law
Beauty is only skin deep, but ugly goes clean to the bone.

Parker's Law of Political Statements
The truth of any proposition has nothing to do with its credibility, and vice versa.

Parker's Rule of Parliamentary Procedure
A motion to adjourn is always in order.

Parkinson's Axioms

1 An official wants to multiply subordinates, not rivals.
2 Officials make work for each other.

Parkinson's First Law
Work expands to fill the time available for its completion; the thing to be done swells in perceived importance and complexity in a direct ratio with the time to be spent in its completion.

Parkinson's Second Law
Expenditure rises to meet income.

Parkinson's Third Law
Expansion means complexity, and complexity decay.

Parkinson's Fourth Law
The number of people in any working group tends to increase regardless of the amount of work to be done.

Parkinson's Fifth Law
If there is a way to delay an important decision, the good bureaucracy, public or private, will find it.

Parkinson's Sixth Law
The progress of science varies inversely with the number of journals published.

Parkinson's Law of Delay
Delay is the deadliest form of denial.

Parkinson's Law for Medical Research
Successful research attracts the bigger grant which makes further research impossible.

Patton's Law
A good plan today is better than a perfect plan tomorrow.

Paulg's Law
In America, it's not how much something costs, it's how much you save.

Peer's Law
The solution to a problem changes the nature of the problem.

Persig's Postulate
The number of rational ways that can explain any given occurrence is infinite.

The Perversity of Nature
You cannot successfully determine beforehand which side of the bread to butter.

The Peter Principle
In a hierarchy, every employee tends to rise to his level of incompetence. This has two corollaries:

1. In time, every post tends to be occupied by an employee who is incompetent to carry out the duties thereof.
2. Work is accomplished by those employees who have not yet reached their level of incompetence.

Peter's Hidden Postulate
Every employee begins at his level of competence.

Peter's Inversion
Internal consistency is valued more highly than efficient service.

Peter's Law of Substitution
Look after the molehills and the mountains will look after themselves.

Peter's Observation
Super-competence is more objectionable than incompetence.

Peter's Placebo
An ounce of image is worth a pound of performance.

Peter's Prognosis
Spend sufficient time confirming the need and the need will disappear.

Peter's Rule for Creative Incompetence
Create the impression that you have already reached your level of incompetence.

Potter's Law
The amount of flak received on any subject is inversely proportional to the subject's true value.

The Probable Dispersal Law
Whatever hits the fan will not be evenly distributed.

The First Law of Procrastination
Procrastination shortens the job and places the responsibility for its termination on someone else – the authority who imposed the deadline.

The Second Law of Procrastination
It reduces anxiety by reducing the expected quality of the project from the best of all possible efforts to the best that can be expected given the limited time.

The Third Law of Procrastination
Status is gained in the eyes of others, and in one's own eyes, because it is assumed that the importance of the work justifies the stress.

The Fourth Law of Procrastination
Avoidance of interruptions, including the assignment of other duties, can usually be achieved, so that the obviously-stressed worker can concentrate on the single effort.

The Fifth Law of Procrastination
Procrastination avoids boredom; one never has the feeling that there is nothing important to do.

The Sixth Law of Procrastination
It may eliminate the job if the need passes before the job can be done.

Pudder's Law
Anything that begins well ends badly.
Anything that begins badly ends worse.

Putt's Law
Technology is dominated by two types of people: those who understand what they do not manage and those who manage what they do not understand.

Rayburn and Dean's Rule
If you want to get along, go along.

Razor Law
The greater the importance of the event being prepared for, the worse the shaving cut.

The First Law of Revision
Changes in design only ever happen once the plans are completed.

The Second Law of Revision
The more innocuous a modification appears to be, the further its influence will extend and the more plans will have to be redrawn.

The Third Law of Revision
Once a design is completed, you will usually find that the measurements are all wrong.

Richard's Rules

1. If you can keep anything long enough, you can throw it away.
2. If you throw anything away, you will need it as soon as it is no longer accessible.

Rosenbaum's Law
The easiest way to find something lost around the house is to buy a replacement.

Ross's Law
Never characterize the importance of a statement in advance.

Rossiter's First Law
Things go wrong.

Rossiter's Second Law
Things are always too complicated.

Rossiter's Third Law
Minor adjustments usually break things. Major adjustments usually break things.

Rossiter's Fourth Law
Nothing works for long.

Rossiter's Accounting Law
In any account, bill or invoice, any error which can creep in will do so. All such errors are never in your favour.

Rossiter's Calendar Law
Important dates are always remembered – the day after they happened.

Rossiter's Car Law
An old car that serves you well will continue to go until four new tyres are put on it.

Rossiter's Dirt Paradox
After you've done the dusting and vacuuming, the furniture and carpets are invariably dustier than when you started.

Rossiter's First Do-it-yourself Law
Easy-to-build do-it-yourself kits usually come without instruction leaflets. If instruction leaflets are supplied, then the instructions will be printed in Japanese or German, never English.

Rossiter's Second Do-it-yoursel Law
All step-ladders are one step too short.

Rossiter's Third Do-it-yourself Law
For any wallpapering job, there's always one roll not enough.

Rossiter's Fourth Do-it-yourself Law
If an object contains two parts, A and B, which have to be fitted together, one or more of these problems will occur:

1 Part A will be missing.
2 Part B will be missing.
3 Both parts will be missing.
4 The connecting bit on part A will be too wide.
5 The connecting bit on part A will not be wide enough.
6 The connecting bit on part B will be too long.
7 The connecting bit on part B will not be long enough.

Rossiter's Fifth Do-it-yourself Law
If a nail is hit with exactly the right amount of force from exactly the right angle, it will bend over. Any deviation from the right amount of force or the right angle will cause the nail to bend over.

Rossiter's Ultimate Do-it-yourself Law
If you want a job doing properly, don't . . .

Rossiter's Gun Law
A Derringer always beats four aces.

Rossiter's Label Law
When all else fails, read the instructions on the label.

Rossiter's Lap Law
When your cat has fallen asleep on your lap and looks utterly content and adorable, you will suddenly have to go to the toilet.

Rossiter's Last Place Statement
You will always find what you arc looking for in the last place you look.

Rossiter's Law of Adjustment
Anything can be made to work if you fiddle with it long enough.

Rossiter's Law of Alcoholic Availability
A pub is always impossible to find when you need a drink.

Rossiter's Law of Anticipation
When given schedules, deadlines or delivery dates, not only should you allow for unexpected delays, but you should also allow for unexpected unexpected delays.

Rossiter's Law of Apertures
Letter boxes are always narrow enough to shred up any newspapers pushed through them.

Rossiter's Law of Appearances
No matter what goes wrong, it will probably look right.

Rossiter's Law of Closure
You only ever run out of cigarettes when all the shops and pubs are closed.

Rossiter's Law of Darkness
Lights only ever fail at night.

Rossiter's Law of Disbelief
Never believe salesmen, advertisements, guarantees, politicians, subordinates, superiors.

Rossiter's Law of Experimentation
No experiment is ever a complete failure – it can always serve as a negative example of something.

Rossiter's Law of Fairness
Any facts which, when included in an argument, give the desired result, are fair facts for the argument.

Rossiter's Law of Foreign Relations
All foreigners are deaf, for they never understand anything you say.

Rossiter's Law of Futility
If it doesn't work first time, forget it. The chances are it'll never work anyway.

Rossiter's Law of Maximum Inaccessibility
If you want something that is stored away, it will be at the bottom of the heap, or at the back of the cupboard, or stashed under everything else.

Rossiter's Law of Mutual Trust
Don't trust anyone.

Rossiter's Law of the Non-guarantee
Warranty and guarantee clauses are voided by non-, partial or total payment of the invoice.

Rossiter's First Law of Opposition
Push something hard enough and it will fall over.

Rossiter's Second Law of Opposition
Push something hard enough and it will break.

Rossiter's Law of Photography
Other people's cameras are impossible to operate.

Rossiter's Law of Precipitation
It always pours with rain the day after you've broken your

umbrella, washed the car, cleaned the windows or painted the gutters.

Rossiter's Library Phenomenon
The book you wanted from the library has been stolen, lost, mislaid or eaten by someone's dog.

Rossiter's Parking Conundrum
Why are car parking spaces always two feet too short?

Rossiter's First Postal Law
Postal deliveries that normally take one day will taken seven days when you are waiting for an important letter.

Rossiter's Second Postal Law
When you have an important letter to post, you will arrive at the postbox three minutes after the last collection.

Rossiter's Queueing Theory
If there is only room for five on a bus, you will be sixth in the queue.

Rossiter's Responsibility Statement
If more than one person is responsible for something, then no-one is at fault when it goes wrong.

Rossiter's Social Law
Social guests always ask for the alcoholic drink that you've got least or none of.

Rossiter's Television Law
Worthwhile television programmes are always shown together at the same time, one on BBC 1, another on ITV, and the third on BBC 2.

Rossiter's Time Quirk
The alarm clock always stops working when you really *do* have to get up early.

Rossiter's Tiredness Paradox
When you feel dog-tired, everyone else is wide-awake; and when you feel wide-awake, everyone else is dog-tired.

Rossiter's Traffic Postulates
When you are in a hurry to get somewhere in your car, traffic lights turn red, traffic jams proliferate, and throngs of pedestrians appear at every zebra crossing.

Rossiter's Transport Theory
Buses, trains and aeroplanes never run late; the timetables are simply optimistic.

Rossiter's Triviality Law
If it takes a certain amount of time to do a large number of trivial tasks, it will invariably take twice as long to do just one more task that is equally trivial.

Rudin's Law
In crises forcing people to choose alternative courses of action, most people will choose the worst possible.

Rule of Accuracy
When working towards the solution of a problem, it always helps if you know the answer.

Runamok's Law
There are four kinds of people: those who sit quietly and do nothing; those who talk about sitting quietly and doing nothing; those who do things; and those who talk about doing things.

Sattinger's Law
It works better if you plug it in.

Schmidt's Law
If you mess about with something long enough, it'll break.

Scott's Law
When an error has been detected and corrected, it will be found

to have been correct in the first place. (This has a corollary: it will then prove impossible to correct the correction.)

Segal's Law
A man with one watch knows what the time is. A man with two watches is never sure.

Law of Selective Gravity
An object will always fall so that it causes maximum damage, both to itself and to the thing it falls on. This has two corollaries:

1. The chance of the bread falling with the buttered side down is directly proportional to the cost of the carpet.
2. The most delicate part will be what drops.

Shanahan's Law
The length of a meeting rises with the square of the number of people present.

Shaw's Principle
Build a system that even a fool can use, and only a fool will want to use it.

Simon's Law
Everything put together falls apart sooner or later; usually sooner.

Skinner's Mathematical Constant
That quantity which, when added to, subtracted from, multiplied by, or divided by the answer you get, gives you the answer which you should have got. (Also known as the **Fudge Factor.**)

Smith's Law
One ought to finish what one starts.

The Snafu Equations

1. The piece of information which is most eagerly sought will not be available.

2 Once you have exhausted all the possibilities and fail, there will be one solution, simple and blindingly obvious, highly visible to everyone else.
3 Badness comes in waves.
4 There's always something missing.

A Law of Socioeconomics
In a hierarchial system, the rate of pay for a given task increases in inverse ratio to the unpleasantness and difficulty of the task.

A Law of Sociogenetics
Celibacy is not hereditary.

Sodd's Law
Sooner or later, the worst possible set of circumstances is bound to occur.

The Spare Parts Principle
The accessibility, during recovery of small parts which fall from the workbench, varies directly with the size of the part, and inversely with its importance to the completion of work in hand.

Spark's Rules for Managers

1 Strive to look tremendously important.
2 Attempt to be seen with important people.
3 Speak with authority; however, only expound on obvious and proven facts.
4 Don't engage in arguments; but, if cornered, ask an irrelevant question and lean back with a satisfied grin while your questioner tries to figure out what's going on – then quickly change the subject.
5 Listen intently while others are arguing the problem. Pounce on a trite statement and bury them with it.
6 If a subordinate asks you a pertinent question, look at him as if he had lost his senses. When he looks down, paraphrase the question back at him.
7 Obtain a brilliant assignment, but keep out of sight and out of the limelight.

8 Walk at a fast pace when out of the office – this keeps questions from subordinates and superiors to a minimum.

9 Always keep the office door closed. This puts visitors on the defensive and also makes it look as if you are always in an important conference.

10 Give all orders verbally. Never write down anything that could possibly be used against you.

Sprinkle's Law

Things always fall from a sufficient height to cause them to break.

Stockmayer's Theorem

If it looks easy, it's tough. If it looks tough, it's damned well impossible.

Sturgeon's Law

Ninety per cent of everything is rubbish.

The Swipple Rule of Order

He who shouts loudest has the floor.

Trischmann's Paradox

A pipe gives a wise man time to think and a fool something to stick in his mouth.

The Law of Triviality

The time spent on any item of the agenda will be in inverse proportion to the sum of money involved.

Truman's Law

If you cannot convince them, confuse them.

Tuccille's Law of Reality

Industry always moves in to fill an economic vacuum.

The Ultimate Principle

By definition, when you are investigating the unknown, you do not know what you will find.

The Unspeakable Law
As soon as you mention something, if it's good, it goes away; if it's bad, it happens.

Wallace's Observation
Everything is in a state of utter dishevelment.

Watson's Law
The reliability of machinery is inversely proportional to the number and significance of any persons watching it.

The Rule of the Way Out
Always leave room to add an explanation if it doesn't work out.

Weiler's Law
Nothing is impossible for the man who doesn't have to do it himself.

Weinberg's First Law
Progress is made on alternate Fridays.

Weinberg's Second Law
If builders built buildings the way computer programmers write computer programmes, then the first woodpecker to come along would destroy civilization.

Weinberg's Corollary
An expert is a person who avoids the small errors while sweeping on to the grand fallacy.

Westheimer's Rule
To estimate the time it takes to do a task: estimate the time you think it should take, multiply by two, and change the unit of measure to the next highest unit. Thus, we allocate two days for a one-hour task.

White's Chappaquiddick Theorem
The sooner and in more detail you announce the bad news, the better.

White's Watergate Theorem
The sooner and in more detail you announce the bad news, the better.

Wiker's Law
Government expands to absorb revenue, and then some.

Williams and Holland's Law
If you collect enough data, you can prove anything by statistical methods.

Workers' Dilemma

1 No matter how much you do, you'll never do enough.
2 What you don't do is always more important than what you do do.

Young's Law
All great discoveries are made by mistake.

THE DEVIL'S MAXIMS

FROM VOLTAIRE TO ROSSITER

Like most actors I am fascinated by words, and I have never known any actors who weren't.

I started to act rather late in life, when I was nearly twenty-seven. I had intended to take a French and German degree course when I came out of the Forces but it wasn't possible because my father had been killed in an air-raid, my mother was on her own, so I couldn't afford to go to university. Instead I went to work in an insurance company. I was there for six and a half years, working in the Claims Department. It really is amazing how many entertainers started life in insurance – and most of them will still try to sell you some, given half a chance.

When I was a child I was very interested in French and had a marvellous French teacher who introduced me to the maxim I remember most clearly from my days at school. It came from Molière: '*Il faut manger pour vivre, non vivre pour manager.*' I thought that was so clever when I was about fourteen. Now I am about forty-four (well, fifty-one actually) my taste in maxims is somewhat more sophisticated.

Anyway, the maxims that follow bring together my interest in words and my interest in insurance; and if you follow all the precepts listed here you will be assured success in all you do. You can even use them when dealing with bores.

Life, alas, is full of boring people, but here is a method of dealing with them. It is simply this: listen to them for a while and then quite deliberately change the subject. In doing so, indicate that you dearly wish you could spend much more time on the first topic (the topic they were boring you with) but that you must talk to them on this other, rather briefer, topic because it's something on which you would so value their opinion. Then all you need to do now is to take one of the maxims below and challenge them with it.

Scrupulous adherence to the code of conduct exemplified in the maxims should endow you with complete health, wealth and happiness because the thoughts that follow represent the distilled wisdom of a score of minds profound – from Voltaire to Rossiter! If, however, you study the maxims and emerge none the wiser, then that is because Voltaire and Rossiter were wrong and Lord Macaulay was right (see page 101) – but still you needn't despair. Once you've learned this chapter by heart you'll always be employable as a Christmas cracker motto-writer. Have fun!

Life is just the interval between birth and death.

All religion is a disease.

Marriage is the only adventure open to the cowardly. **Voltaire**

Some people are so immune to gossip that if they were dead, they'd be the last to know it.

Adults are obsolete children. **Dr Seuss**

Almost anything can be accomplished, if you don't care who gets the credit for it.

Every fool wants to give advice.

If you have to make a decision in a hurry, 'No' is always a better answer than 'Yes', for 'No' can be more easily changed to 'Yes' later on, than 'Yes' to 'No'.

A man's worst difficulty is that he has freedom of choice.

Lots of people confess to little faults – to suggest that they have no big ones.

The source of all contradiction is the brain of civilized man.

Never trust a man who speaks well of everybody. **John Churton Collins**

The Universe is just one of God's practical jokes.

God moves in very mysterious ways – he never leaves any fingerprints!

Everyone dislikes something about their own body.

Middle age is when you meet so many people that every new person you meet reminds you of someone else, and usually is. **Ogden Nash**

Bureaucracy is the rule of nobody in particular.

The worst thing about being buried is being buried alive.

A fool is his own informer.

Every year the English winter ends in July and recommences in August.

Nature has given women so much power that the law has very wisely given them little. **Dr Johnson**

Cigarettes are killers that travel in packs. **Mary Ott**

It's easy to be an angel when nobody ruffles your feathers.

It's strange that anyone should turn to crime when there are so many legal ways to be dishonest.

The more things a man is ashamed of, the more respectable he is. **George Bernard Shaw**

At all costs, arguments are to be avoided – they can often be convincing.

All is unfair in love and war.

To get to know a friend properly, you must share an inheritance with him.

We only forgive when it suits us.

You can only make jokes about good religions.

Every luxury must be paid for, and everything is a luxury. **Cesare Pavese**

Honesty is the best policy?

Honesty is often the worst policy.

There is no-one so rich that he does not still want everything.

The majority is never right.

No party is as bad as its leaders. **Will Rogers**

If you want something tested to see if it really works, begin by offering it to someone else as advice.

Aristocracy is just another name for well-organized bad manners.

Very few people's expressions and words ever coincide.

To say that you can love one person all your life is just like saying that one candle will continue burning as long as you live. **Leo Tolstoy**

Silence is often the cruellest liar.

Even if you chop off the head of the Devil, evil will still remain.

Everything has a use – even uselessness itself.

Everything has a use – if only we could think of it.

I believe the best definition of man is the ungrateful biped. **Feodor Dostoevski**

Fine minds don't always make fine people.

Mary had a little lamb – the midwife fainted.

If at first you don't succeed, give up.

You start dying the minute you are born.

Bad excuses are worse than none.

The behaviour of many children suggests that their parents embarked on the sea of matrimony without a paddle.

We have all forgotten more than we remember.

Don't look back in anger – look forward in fury.

April Fools have a day all their own; the rest of us have to muddle along without any recognition at all.

A miracle is a natural law that happens once.

Universal advice to the engaged: disengage.

Fashion is just a clothing epidemic.

The only thing that experience teaches us is that experience teaches us nothing. **André Maurois**

Any place in Britain to which everyone can go cannot possibly be respectable.

Religion is the masterpiece of the art of animal training, for it trains people as to how they shall think. **Arthur Schopenhauer**

My mind is already made up. Don't confuse me with facts!

Hope sometimes triumphs over experience – look at the number of people who remarry.

If there were no bad people, there would be no good lawyers. **Charles Dickens**

Even the world's most arch despiser esteems himself as a self-despiser.

Do other men, as they would do you.

It is because of men that women dislike one another. **Jean de La Bruyère**

If you marry and get a good wife, you'll be happy; if you marry and get a bad wife, you'll become a philosopher. **Socrates**

Life is one big maze, and most people take a wrong turning fairly early in life.

If you're not part of the solution, then you must be part of the problem.

People are governed by the brain; a tender heart is of no value to someone who wants to win.

There are some people so addicted to exaggeration that they can't tell the truth without lying. **Josh Billings.**

The greatest mischief you can do the envious is to do well.

The irritating thing about love is that it is a crime calling for an accomplice.

More people would be cowards if they had courage enough to be.

One good deed has a multitude of claimants.

People would be more inclined to throw out unwanted articles if they didn't think that someone might pick them up and find a use for them.

History is just prophecy backward.

Invalids live the longest.

When a proud man hears another praised, he thinks himself injured.

Whisky is the most popular of all the cold cures that don't work.

No-one minds a man being clever, so long as he keeps it to himself.

Everybody calls 'clear' those ideas which have the same degree of confusion as his own. **Marcel Proust**

You never know how dirty your hands are until you peel a hard-boiled egg.

No-one knows what he can't do until he tries and fails.

However absurd something may seem, someone's bound to have said it before.

Everybody wants to be somebody; nobody wants to become somebody.

Early to bed,
Early to rise,
These are the reasons
Why a man dies.

Experience is just another name for the mistakes that a person makes.

A thief is just a person with a fine eye for opportunity.

Everyone complains that cards are poorly shuffled, until they get good hands.

Politeness is a pleasant way for a man to get nowhere with a girl.

Everybody is ignorant, only on different subjects. **Will Rogers**

Courtesy is a form of polite behaviour practised by civilized people when they have time.

Very few men are eager to accept good advice, for it usually interferes with their plans.

When I first started working, I used to dream of the day when I would earn the salary I starve on now.

The Devil will not come into Cornwall, for fear of being put into a pie. (*Old Cornish proverb arising from the fact that Cornish people will put almost anything into a pie.*)

The loudest voice often wins the quarrel.

Youth is a blunder; manhood a struggle; old age a regret. **Benjamin Disraeli**

Sleep faster, we need the pillows. (*Yiddish proverb.*)

Life would just about be tolerable were it not for its intolerableness.

When in doubt, leave it out.

How can anyone know what they think until they open their mouth and hear what they say?

The most bigoted of all people are those without any convictions.

Don't listen to reason – reason is only what other people have to say.

To tell a child what it may not do is to tell it what it will do.

When God created the Universe, he also created 'error' – that was a mistake.

What you don't know won't hurt you; who you don't know might!

In order to remember it, everyone has to change the truth a little.

If soldiers were asked to do in battle what the average motorist does at weekends for fun, the officer in charge would be court-martialled for brutality. **Malcolm Muggeridge**

Ask a man for his opinion of women in general – his answer will tell you a lot about his wife.

If you think you've seen the writing on the wall, beware! It may be a forgery.

Most women are not so young as they are painted. **Max Beerbohm**

Some people are capable of so misunderstanding that they do not even get hold of the wrong end of the stick – they get hold of the wrong stick.

A woman shows more taste in her choice of underwear than in her choice of jewellery.

Other people are only to be taken in small doses.

A passionate belief in democracy makes it impossible for any democratic institution to function properly.

Even before it happens, the anarchist will be disappointed with the future.

Criticism is the disapproval of people, not for having faults, but for having faults different from our own.

There's always another crisis around the corner. **Harry Truman**

Indifference to what the newspapers say is a prerequisite for those who govern.

Doctors make the worst patients.

So heavy is the chain of wedlock that it needs two to carry it, and sometimes three. **Alexandre Dumas**

Mythology is just gossip grown old.

Of all sexual aberrations, perhaps the most peculiar is chastity. **Rémy de Gourmont**

Give a thief enough rope, and he'll steal it!

Anyone possessing the merest amount of originality is usually called a crank by his fellow creatures.

A kiss that speaks volumes is seldom a first edition. **Clare Whiting**

Prejudice is a great saver of time – you can form opinions without bothering to get the facts.

A likely impossibility is always preferable to an unconvincing possibility. **Aristotle**

History is ninety per cent criminal.

Is it progress if a cannibal uses a knife and fork? **Stanislaus Lec**

He who fondles you more than usual has either deceived you or wants to do so.

When passions run high, reason runs low.

A man may be a fool and not know it – but not if he is married.
H. L. Mencken

Money is the root of all good.

Money is the fruit of most evil.

The impossibility of yesterday has become the luxury of today and the necessity of tomorrow.

Silence is obsolete.

Familiarity breeds attempt.

Familiarity breeds children.

Familiarity breeds.

When a man likes to have a ball without the chain, that's a bachelor.

The public is not really concerned about fallout from nuclear explosions; so far it hasn't affected television reception.

If God meant people to go nude, they would have been born that way.

Bad habits are like a comfortable bed – easy to get into, hard to get out of. **Watson Black**

Men only ever devote their enthusiasm, time and energy to matters in which their passions have a personal interest.

Necessity is the mother of crafty dodges.

That period of history which is most obscure is today.

A deaf husband and a blind wife always make a happy couple.

Generals cannot be entrusted with anything, not even with war. **Georges Clemenceau**

Practical politics is the art of ignoring the obvious facts.

Not only is there no God, try getting a plumber at weekends.

Life is just a bowl of cherries – pips lurking everywhere.

Life is just like a dream – but don't wake me. (*Yiddish proverb*)

Bridge, probably because of its tendency to encourage prolonged smoking, and its deadly immobility, is the most dangerous game played in England now.

Some people never learn anything because they understand everything too soon.

Take care to get what you like or you will be forced to like what you get. **George Bernard Shaw**

Conversation is a form of communication in which many people never stop to think and many others never think to stop.

One has to be as cautious in telling the truth as in concealing it.

Women inspire men to great things, yet prevent them from achieving those same things.

Lazy people have no spare time. (*Japanese proverb*)

Imagination is what makes you think you're having a good time when all you're really doing is spending money.

The Bible tells us to love our neighbours, and also to love our enemies; probably because they are generally the same people. **G. K. Chesterton**

Less of your courtesy and more of your purse.

Every man has his price – it's just a question of determining it.

All New Year Resolutions are made to be broken.

We are all capable of evil thoughts, but only very rarely of evil deeds; we can all do good deeds, but very few of us can think good thoughts. **Cesare Pavese**

Reason has made mankind forget his emotion.

Good wine ruins the pocket; bad wine ruins the stomach.

If the art of conversation stood a little higher, we would have a lower birthrate. **Stanislaus Lec**

He who commences many things finishes few.

When in doubt, tell the truth. **Mark Twain**

Nothing difficult is ever easy.

What makes everyone discontented with their condition is their absurdly exaggerated idea of the happiness of others.

When a diplomat says yes, he means perhaps; when he says perhaps, he means no; and when he says no, he is no diplomat.

Human history becomes more and more a race between education and catastrophe. **H. G. Wells**

If the rich could hire other people to die for them, the poor could make a wonderful living. (*Yiddish proverb*)

The wise man knows that he knows nothing; the fool believes that he knows everything.

When you think you've seen the light at the end of the tunnel, take care. It's probably a train coming from the opposite direction.

Wine is a simple but elegant means of getting tight.

I know I am among civilized men because they are fighting so savagely. **Voltaire**

Whatever is not nailed down is mine; whatever I can pry loose is not nailed down.

No man but a blockhead ever wrote, except for money. **Dr Johnson**

Nostalgia ain't what it used to be.

In time, today will be thought of as part of the Dark Ages.

Nicotine is great for killing people.

He who talks to himself, talks to a fool.

If I dealt in candles, the sun would never set. (*Yiddish proverb*)

It's true that money talks. It usually says 'Goodbye'.

Mistrust simplicity.

All mental activity is easy, as long as it doesn't have to take account of reality.

It's hard to believe that a man is telling the truth when you know that you would lie if you were in his place. **H. L. Mencken**

Religion is man using a divining rod. Philosophy is man using a pick and shovel.

Once-powerful adjectives have been made meaningless by the world of advertising.

The greatest distinguishing feature between men and animals is the former's desire to take medicine.

Bibo ergo sum – I drink, therefore I am.

Sometimes I think, therefore sometimes I am.

I don't think, therefore . . .

Any fool can tell the truth, but it requires a man of some sense to know how to lie well. **Samuel Butler (II)**

I don't mind liars, but I do hate people who are inaccurate.

Yesterday's proof is today's imagination.

A wise man knows everything; a shrewd one, everybody.

A man cannot be too careful in the choice of his enemies. **Oscar Wilde**

Clever liars give details, but the cleverest liars don't.

Many people are thought brave because they are scared to run away.

Do not do unto others as you would that they should do unto you. Their tastes may not be the same. **George Bernard Shaw**

The Eleventh Commandment: thou shalt not get found out.

The Twelfth Commandment: if found out, thou shalt not get caught.

Inventions were much easier in the past. Modern man is running out of things to invent.

All original ideas are dangerous to the existing order of things.

He who indulges, bulges. **Eleanor Rydberg**

No man or woman was made wretched in a brothel – they were that way when they entered.

Any offensive object, placed at a proper distance, attains a degree of beauty.

The occasional lie sometimes saves long-drawn out explanations.

When love seems imminent, take a fortnight's holiday – alone.

If you want to drown yourself, make sure the water's deep enough.

If a thing is worth doing, someone is bound to screw it up.

Self-interest is often disguised as disinterestedness.

Passion often turns the wisest men into fools, and makes the greatest asses wise.

The purpose of speech is to conceal thought.

Social climbing is the art of stepping on the right people.

Fanaticism consists in redoubling your effort when you have forgotten your aim. **George Santayana**

Every man thinks himself superior to his equals.

Virtue is more enjoyable when a man repents his faults rather than avoiding them.

The man who loves himself has one big advantage over the man who loves someone else – he won't encounter many rivals for his love.

A pessimist is someone who has had to live with an optimist.

The world gets better every day – and much worse every night.

If God lived on earth, people would break his windows.

The only cure for mental anguish is physical pain.

A consultant is the person called in when nobody wants to take the blame for what's going wrong.

Half-truth – whole lie. (*Yiddish proverb*.)

One great mistake made by intelligent persons is to refuse to believe that people are as stupid as they are. **Marquise de Tencin**

Conviction is strongest when knowledge is least.

The only business in the world where the amateurs are better than the professionals is prostitution.

The trouble with being punctual is that there's nobody there to appreciate it. **Lettice Philpots**

In any argument, the man with the greater intelligence is always wrong, because he did not use his intelligence to avoid the argument in the first place.

If you spend all your life working towards a particular goal, be careful. Make sure no-one moves the goal-posts at the last minute.

Old age won't catch on – there's not much future in it.

Be suspicious of people who are indignant.

Man cannot be a reasonable animal, for he always loses his temper when he is called upon to act in accordance with the dictates of reason.

Many prejudices are well-founded.

Those who do not complain are never pitied. **Jane Austen**

Doing easily what others find difficult is talent; doing what is impossible is genius.

The difference between gossip and news depends on whether you hear it or tell it.

A human being is an ingenious assemblage of portable plumbing. **Christopher Morley**

All faults are more pardonable than the methods used to hide them.

Conscience is often an anticipation of other people's opinions.

Liars need good memories.

The English have an extraordinary ability for flying into a great calm. **Alexander Woollcott**

Never let your schooling interfere with your education.

Man was not God's best idea – even God had his off-days.

It's hard to know where one generation ends and the next one begins – but it's somewhere round nine o'clock at night. **Charles Ruffing**

He who gambles picks his own pocket.

No drunk of any standing is to be found in the gutter.

A man never cheats anyone but himself.

If we had everything we wanted, we wouldn't like what we had. **William Feather**

If all politicians were laid end to end, they wouldn't reach any conclusion.

Everybody should believe in something. I believe I'll have another drink.

There is nothing so useless as doing efficiently that which should not be done at all. **Peter Drucker**

'Know thyself', said the philosopher – but if most people really knew themselves, they'd run a mile.

Refined manners make for unhappy people.

Those who do not feel pain seldom think that it is felt. **Dr Johnson**

Keep a thing seven years and you will find a use for it.

The future is no longer what it used to be. **Friedrich Hollander**

Nothing is more injurious to the intellect than one's emotions in full flight.

Nothing changes.

The thought of suicide is a great comfort to the depressed.

Natural man has just two basic desires: to get and to beget.

How come if God is so all-powerful and omnipotent that he's got such a short name? **Nina Weisman**

Adolescence is the age when a girl's voice changes from no to yes.

Never lift a stone merely to drop it on your own toe.

The best way to be boring is to leave nothing out. **Voltaire**

If ignorance is bliss, why aren't more people happy?

The best and cheapest oral contraceptive: No!

The first breath is the beginning of death.

Wild horses couldn't drag a secret out of most women. Unfortunately, women seldom have lunch with wild horses. **Ivern Boyett**

In a democracy, the votes of the vicious and stupid count. But under any other system, they might be running the show.

No man is exempt from saying silly things; the mischief is to say them deliberately. **Michel de Montaigne**

The best defence against a nuclear bomb is not to be there when it goes off.

Nothing is so useless as a general maxim. **Lord Macaulay**